YWM²

You're worth much more.

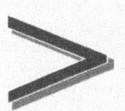

WRITTEN BY

Sheri Asuoha

YWM²: You're Worth Much More. Copyright© 2021 by Sheri Asuoha

All rights reserved. This book is protected by the copyright laws of the United States of America. This book may not be copied or reprinted for commercial gain or profit. The use of short quotations, or occasional page copying for personal, or groups study is permitted and encouraged. Permission will be granted upon request unless otherwise identified. Please do not participate in or encourage piracy of copyrighted materials in violation of the author's rights. Purchase only authorized editions.

Scripture quotations are from the New Living Translation© Copyright 1982 by Thomas Nelson, Inc©.

Use by permission all rights reserved.

This Book and other publications by the author are available at all major bookstores and book outlets nationwide.

ISBN: 9781737786405

Publisher: 7th Seal Advantage, LLC
Content Editor: Cherie Animashaun
Copy Editor: Olubukola Adebayo | Ariwa Consulting
Cover Page: MidoDezines

*This book is dedicated
to anyone who was ever told
they were not enough.*

{Contents}

Foreword..1

Math...3

1. Letter to a Suicidal Generation 21
2. The Art of the Cry 52
3. How Not to Drown in Troubled Waters 73
4. There's Nothing Wrong with You.................... 83
5. Learning to Walk... 107
6. Learning to Fight 120
7. Stewardship.. 135
8. Stewardship II: YWM² 156

Aftermath. 179

Afterword 197

About The Author..199

{Foreword}

Beloved, how do you feel about yourself? What do you think about your life? Ask this of yourself. Ask this of the young people in your life, especially your children. I need you to understand that poverty of the soul is real, and it is lethal. What makes you believe you are less than life? What makes you think God made a mistake in provoking your existence and sustaining it for as long as He has? What makes you think you don't have what it takes to make it in life? Poverty of the soul. It is the cause of much loss, heartbreak, and frustration in children of God and in those called to be God's children but don't know it yet.

Many people complain about what they are lacking when the truth is, they had what they needed, but lost it after they allowed poverty to make its bed in their lives. It's this same poverty that renders intelligent people ignorant and unable to make wholesome decisions. An impoverished soul tells a person all about who they are not and what they do not have, causing them to make the wrong decisions in life and skip all the required processes that would have made them unstoppable forces and change agents on the earth. If you are a parent, do not find yourself going in circles all because we refuse to acknowledge and part with generational and cultural lies. Ignoring areas where healing and deliverance is needed provides a gateway to a poverty that has been custom designed by the perpetuation of demonic lies.

Parents...children... EVERYONE: consciously seek the truth about your identity and capacity. Children are limitless under God if we as parents will cooperate with Him. You are limitless, too if you will partner with your Creator. This book must be a part of your bookshelf. Once you finish it, reread it and distribute it until the world knows they are worth much more.

- Rev. Adesola Babalola, FNP-BC

Math.

"Black kids don't do well in math. Especially not the girls." I don't know where I first heard this. But by 7th grade, I had definitely internalized it. That was the first time I had seen an 'A' on any math related assignment in years and I could not believe it. In fact, I refused to.

In the first quarter of 4th grade, I received my first 'C'. From there on, every grade of that nature became acceptable by my parent's and even by my own standards. I was surprised I didn't get in trouble for bringing home that "C" in fourth grade. But I did get something worse.

What About My Grade?

That day, at the end of the first quarter of the fourth grade, my mother walked into my grandmother's living room with my report card after parent-teacher conferences. She also held my siblings' report cards in her hand. We all ran to greet her. I stopped short of hugging her and took a seat on the stairs watching my mother and siblings smother one another with flagrant displays of affection I didn't fully understand.

I took in the scenery. My Grandmother's living room was quite elaborate. It was clean and bright. The carpet was the brightest shade of ivory and soft, topped with imported ebony and oriental furnishings. A velvet couch accented the space. We were seldom allowed to frequent the living room. But this day was an exception.

Typically on report card day and other special days when we had something to brag about, we gathered around the oriental coffee table, the children would sit amongst the accent pillows or if we were lucky, on one of the special oriental stools we could pull out from under the coffee table. The adults sat on the big furniture and the velvet couch. They would sit there discussing the implication of our various successes and achievements and how they knew I would be a doctor one day.

"Mommy! Mommy! How did I do?" squealed my younger sister.

YWM²

"Am I in trouble?" My little brother asked appropriately.

My mother gave him a look that implied what she was too annoyed to verbalize, giving him all the information he needed to know to keep his distance. My brother, Chris, was notorious for behaving in ways no man could explain.

"What about me, Mommy?" My little sister inquired again.

"You actually did very well," she looked at my sister, charmed by the delighted grin on the little struggle reader's kindergarten face.

"And Chris," she glared, "Your grades are actually pretty good, too!" He did not see that coming. None of us did. "They said he's really smart, he just…" Mommy reported to the other adults in the room.

Hmm. She had been in the house at least three minutes by now and nothing had been said of my brilliance, off-the-chart test scores, recommendations for transfer into gifted programs or anything. Maybe because I hadn't asked. I'd barely even greeted my mother beyond brief eye contact and a slight smile acknowledging her return.

Sheri Asuoha

My demeanor in those days was as limited as my credit score would be by age 25. Stifling. Despite how unbothered I presented, I was actually very excited about my mother's return from parent-teacher conferences because as flawed as my personality was, academics and any form of public performance was my time to shine above and beyond my more likeable, energetic sibling counterparts. So, when I noticed my mother had yet to provide me with the opportunity to show off my humility and poise, I thought, *Hmm. I'll have to incite it then.*

"Mommy, what about my grades?" I asked in sheepish confidence. She paused, taking a breath, as if she needed time to find the words…and I wished I hadn't asked.

"I actually thought you would do better," she replied, handing me my report card as she turned to inform the other adults in the room about my… 'C'.

What on earth is a 'C'? Is it… some kind of regular, ungifted person's mark? Is she sure these aren't my sibling's grades? I struggled to conceptualize what a 'C' was and what it meant about me, but I knew what it wasn't: anything to brag about.

I'd looked forward to report card day all week in anticipation of the much needed validation. Instead came the day I internalized that there was now nothing special about me.

That day, it was resolved by me and the family elders that the 'C' I earned was consistent with my capacity. The dreams of me being a doctor, diminished.

I could not believe. But eventually, I learned to accept it as my truth. There was a time when I could NEVER arrive home with such a mark and live to tell the story.

I Bring the A's Home

The first time I brought anything less than 'A' to my mother's home, I was in 1st grade. My teacher was Ms. Jones. I was really proud because Ms. Jones had placed a glistening sticker in the shape of a star just to the left of a big red 'B⁺'. I was excited to see a different letter for a change. I proudly showed Mommy my graded paper.

I was grinning from ear to ear. I can never forget the look on her face when she told me, "This is the last time you ever bring home anything like this," If you listened carefully, you could hear my proud grin shatter to the ground in millions of pieces. I quickly replaced it with shame. Shame and I became the best of friends and would be so for years to come. Shame and Sheri. Sheri and shame.

"You bring home 'A's' and 'A+'s'. Not 'A-' or 'B' or any other letter, do you understand me?"

"Yes Ma'am," I understood, I think.

A month or so later, towards the end of the school year, my grandmother picked me up from school while my mom was at work. She wanted to see my desk. As it is today- depending on which of my offices you visit, my desk was scattered and filled with papers and notes. You might call it messy. I called it the desk of someone getting things done. You're right. It was messy.

"What's all this?" my grandmother asked, sifting through all the papers in my desk.

"This is my scratch paper. This is my artwork. It's abstract and also cat. These are the graded homework papers I wanted to keep, but I can't take them home."

YWM²

Of course, she sifts through all my graded papers. Why she couldn't just focus on my abstract cat is beyond me.

"Sherilynn, these are really good grades! Look at all these 'A-'s' and 'B+'s'!" She was kind enough not to mention the 'B-' I am sure she saw. *She knows the truth about me. She will never look at me the same again. She will tell my mother…* I or maybe Shame told myself. Shame and Sheri- together, again.

"I didn't do well on those," I admitted, under Shame's instruction, my head bowed towards hell. Shame and Sheri. Sheri and shame. *Shame, meet my grandmother. She is amazing! A shame, she will never look at me the same way again… And she's going to tell my mother.*

"Granddaughter, you're so smart. Look! This one has a smiley face! So does this one! Let's bring them home so your mother can see all your smiley faces. We can put them on your refrigerator…"

I knew she planned to tell my mother. I could not let that happen. We looked Grandmother dead in the eyes, Shame and me. "We don't bring home 'B's'. We don't' bring home 'A-'s'". I bring the 'A's' home only.

Mommy doesn't want to see any other letters." I snatched and shredded every graded paper and proceeded to gather my belongings and clean out my desk as if everything happening was normal and Ms. Jones wasn't staring at my dysfunction from a distance. "We can throw them all away. I don't know why I was saving them."

I saved the 'B-' because I could not figure out why I didn't get a smiley face on that one. What was I doing wrong? All I knew is if I brought home those bad grades, Mommy would find out I was as bad as they were. She would learn I was not as smart as she thought I was. So I had to hide them.

*As an aside, that demonic logic developed into a mindset I carried for some time. Deceit and inauthenticity became my second nature. If I decided anything was wrong with me or my experiences, I learned to hide them and only communicate what I thought was acceptable.

But as I mentioned earlier, the day came when 'B-'s' and even 'C's' were acceptable. No one expected me to be smart anymore. So that helped. Right?

YWM²

Not Math

In 7th grade, my math and homeroom teacher, Ms. Williams, announced the unexpected: "...It does not matter what you get right or wrong," she stated louder than necessary. "Whoever completes this entire math packet within the hour does not have to do any math homework the rest of the week." *Say what?* I thought to myself. "All I ask," she continued, "...is that you do your absolute best. And trust me, I will know if you tried."

Say less. I sat down, focused (something I rarely did) and completed my pre-algebra packet, mostly estimating/guessing within the hour. The teacher eventually collected the packets from those of us brave enough to take on the challenge. She started grading mine immediately.

"Mrs. Williams, you said it didn't matter if we were right..."

"I know what I said," sassy Black lady teacher, she was. She looked at me, "You didn't copy this from the back of the..." then she remembered who she was talking to, "You lost your textbook". She rolled her eyes.

"I lost my textbook," I confirmed in sync with her. I lost that joker weeks ago.

I was always losing things. That year alone, I lost assignments. Textbooks. My clarinet. My mind. That habit lasted well into adulthood. Remind me to tell you about the time I lost my keys.

Ms. Williams looked through my packet once more. "Yep. These are all correct," she informed me. "Seriously? All of them?" I asked in disbelief.

"Yep, let me show this to Mr. Clifton," she walked out of the class and across the hall, to talk to Mr. Clifton, the teacher of the gifted students (the white kids). *Did she just leave us, a classroom of 7th graders to our own devices so she can gossip about me to the old white man across the hall?* When she returned, I was asked to stay after school to meet with Mr. Clifton.

"How did you get this answer?" He asked me. I showed him. "That makes sense, but can you try doing it this way?" he asked. I panicked. *Is this old white man trying to teach me math? Does he not see me?* Mr. Clifton asked me again when I took too long to respond. *Wow, he is really trying to teach me math.* I chuckled.

YWM²

"Mr. Clifton, I may talk white, but as you can see… *I am about to waste your time, sir… I thought silently. He must know he's being ridiculous. We both know I can't do this.* I said to myself regarding the pre-algebra packet I just received %100 on.

"Okay. I did not ask your race. I asked you to try solving this problem this way." Clearly, he had no sense of humor.

Finally, I answered him, "I don't even understand what you're asking me to do right now. I am not good at math."

"It's okay," he responded, "You look like you're about to cry. There's nothing to be sad about," he looked at me compassionately. I was not used to that at all. I instantly became uncomfortable with the idea of someone seeing my feelings and responding to them. My defenses began to rise along with my body temperature. "I know it seems hard," he continued, "But I think you can do it. Just try. Do you want me to show you again?"

I remember looking into his bifocal-covered, green eyes. The look he gave me was so foreign, I couldn't interpret it. I decided he was a threat. Looking back, his eyes were not threatening at all. They were attentive and caring. It totally freaked me out.

"I'm not crying. It's my sinuses. I'm allergic to this entire situation and your beard, Mr. Clause, I mean Mr. Clifton" He put his pencil down and took his bifocals off.

"Ms. Williams thinks you should be in the accelerated math program. I'm willing to work with you to catch up to where we are, but... is this too much for you?"

"Yes, "I answered without hesitation. "I would love to be in all the accelerated everything. But I am slow. I am only good at reading and writing, sometimes, but usually I don't even know what's going on" I laughed.

"Okay. Come back when you are ready to try," he instructed as he escorted me out. I guess he was mad about the "beard" comment.

I wondered if Ms. Williams lied about me getting those answers right. Maybe she just didn't want me in her class. She was always annoyed with me. I lost my textbook. I was convinced that the only reason she did not tell my mother is because she thought I was being abused at home and didn't want the extra work of having to report it if I came to school all bruised up.

YWM²

You Guessed It

About a decade later, I found myself applying for a master's program. I never planned to get a masters. I barely knew what one was but apparently, they were all the rage amongst my very "woke" peers and boyfriend at the time. He refused to stay with me if I didn't attend graduate school. I had to take the GRE. I expected to epically fail the math portion, but balance things out with a killer score in writing with hopes of getting into somebody's grad school and maintaining my relationship status.

To my surprise, I was average in the essay writing. Just average?! The shade! But even more of a surprise- my highest scores were in all the quantitative sections. All of them. The scores were very, very high- at least for me. I couldn't believe it. I was so excited I immediately called my boo. "Wow. You must have guessed really well," he responded. I hadn't seen Shame since she escorted me from his (or someone's) dorm room one morning. Shame and Sheri were together once more. *Maybe I had guessed really well.*

I guessed so well on that test I was offered scholarships to three different graduate programs in fields like business and... engineering. *Engineering?* I thought. *What do I look like driving a train ... or fixing buildings. Or whatever engineers do with their math.* This was the extent of my understanding of engineering at the time.

One of the offers I received was a full ride to a business college in Ohio and the other two were to the University of Illinois and the University of Illinois in Champaign- Urbana for their engineering programs.

I ignored all those offers. U of I in Champaign-Urbana, chased me for a full year, disturbing me to apply and accept a scholarship for their program. I guess they needed more Black women. *Good luck finding us*, I thought. *Crazy recruiters...they fell for my lucky guesses that I'd worked so hard to solve.* Idiot, Idiot, Idiot... as Grandmother would say.

I was the idiot. Less, than a year later, I paid $250,000 to get my master's degree in clinical counseling... to be an entry level case manager making less than $35k annually.

I was told Black girls were smart enough to be nurses at best. But if you couldn't, then your next option was social worker, or some form of stripper. I didn't like needles and I ate far too many donuts to be the latter.

If I understood the salary distinction between the hard and the soft sciences - even if it was all lucky guesses that got me in the door, I could have lucky guessed my way right into a free Master's in Engineering. You bought this book for what, $10 on Amazon? If this was an engineering textbook, it would cost $10 to preview a sample of the most interesting engineering textbook you'll have ever read. What a difference it makes to know the WORTH of something!

Poverty of the Soul

My pastor did a series once. He called it, *Poverty of the Soul*. He is going to let me talk about it here for free because he loves me, but it won't do that series any justice. If he writes the book, I encourage you to buy it. In this series, he explained to us that our souls are purposed to prosper, citing 3 John 1:2:

> *Beloved, I pray that you may prosper in all things and be in health, just as your soul prospers.*
>
> ***3 John 1:2***

He then explains the downhill spiral that ensues when we fail to identify the purpose and value of our souls.

"Revelation. Information. Interpretation," he said in his thick, Yoruba accent. "Think about what each of these words means… you need all of them if you plan to be wealthy in life," I thought about my life so far with regard to these three words. By now, Pastor would have drawn out a graph illustrating the correlative relationship between revelation, information and interpretation. See how the information I allowed myself to take in overtime dictated how I interpreted both the negative and positive situations I experienced in my early years?

I don't think I fully understood the definition of the word 'bastard' until I gained revelational knowledge of who Satan truly is. He is a bully and a coward who imposes his father-lacking, identity crisis bearing issues on everyone he feels threatened by. You do not have to be a victim to Satan's bullying tactics.

Whatever it is you think your being is worth, forget it. You are worth much more. Nobody invests in the mass production of something that lacks value. But

YWM[2]

God's first commandment to you was, "Be fruitful and multiply[1]," that was in the Old Testament. In the New Testament, He tells us to "Go out and make disciples[2]" Again, He introduces this concept of replication, this time by way of discipleship.

As you have already seen, this book is full of my personal business, random anecdotes, a few rants and a lot of scripture- not because I have nothing better to do. If I wrote this book well, not only will you do everything to preserve and maximize your value here and on earth, but you will also replicate all the best and most divine parts of you in others. If I wrote this well- and by well, I mean exactly as the Holy Spirit instructed, then you will never try to hide any part of your life. You won't deny your past. You will believe your life and future is as glorious as the God you serve, and you'll surrender it all to Him so He can show you how to profit from it.

At the very least, by the end of this book you should be inspired to see value in all of your experiences- including those you overlooked. You should see the value in the people God has placed around you.

---

[1] Genesis 1:28
[2] Matthew 28:19

Sheri Asuoha

Are you familiar with Philippians 4:19?

And my God will supply all your needs according to the riches of his glory in Christ Jesus.

You probably get hype just knowing "...God will supply all your needs..." And that's cool. But if you get to the end of this book, the information you take in will make this scripture hit different. Wait 'til you find out you're too valuable to be the recipient; He had to make you part of the metric by which He blesses the world. Let that sink in, Riches of His Glory (My new nickname for you). Be blessed as you read.

{1}

Letter to a Suicidal Generation

...Don't be a fool! Why die before your time?
Ecclesiastes 7:17

A few years ago, I met this guy. Smart. Driven. Handsome, too... with great credit and even great ideas. One day, we took a walk. I thought it might be nice if we could take in the sun and Chicago cool while we enjoyed one another's company. So, we found a safe, quiet neighborhood and we walked. He was telling me how much he admired and enjoyed talking to me while I pretended that was something I heard all the time.

Turn Up for Your Birthday

"Me?" I chuckled. "You're the one to be admired. I wish I had your drive. Look at everything you've accomplished – and in a pandemic! Meanwhile, I am still working on my goals from 2012! You're the G.O.A.T, bro. You, my friend, are the admirable one."

He smiled. "My life is going really well, I suppose... better than I thought it would, honestly," His blueish green eyes glistening in the sunlight as we walked. His face had been so serious the past few moments we had been talking. He walked, as if on eggshells. I decided to slow my pace. Maybe that would encourage him to be easy. When he noticed the intentionality in my change of pace, he looked at me- maybe to see what I was noticing about him. I smiled to let him know he had done nothing wrong and that he was safe.

My face was full of strength and joy, unspeakable. But I understood how heavy his face felt. I understood how, even when things were going well, you never knew how long it would last. I was confident that if I could keep his attention, my joy had to rub off on him. It did. Finally, his tense disposition began to soften- his face melting into a mild and sheepish grin, something I could tell his face had not felt in a long time.

"I have really amazing credit now," he changed the subject. "I can get a place wherever I want. I can buy a house. That's crazy. Just last year, I was basically homeless. I can't believe they kicked me out... kept all my money. But you know how it is, right?"

"Yeah," I shared, reflectively. "Robbie, it took the Father, Son, Holy Spirit and most of His angels to pull me out the gutter," I laughed, answering him truthfully. "I had to make a lot of sacrifices, too. I had to decide what was most important for my life and give up things that I really loved for what I knew would give my life meaning and substance, you know?"

The sheepish grin of his faded away. "See! I knew you were about to make this spiritual. God this and God that. You kill me with that," he shot, catching me (almost) off guard. I saw where this was headed from the start.

"You think you're the only one who knows God? You think I don't? I pray to Him every day. I accepted Jesus and His ways whether He accepts me or not. He should accept me! He made me like this! It's His fault I am how I am."

I hadn't stopped smiling. I stopped walking and so did he. I gave him my full attention as he continued to speak.

"I... I don't think I'm doing anything wrong," he started. "I like guys. I have better relationships with them. It's easier with them, too, you know. I am a good person." He spurted defensively, his eyes seeking validation that both he and I knew wasn't my place to give him. The only thing I could validate for him was his feelings.

"Robbie, I spent like 10 minutes telling you how admirable you are. Why would you suggest anything to the contrary? I was simply sharing my experience in response to your question about my life. I was being as honest with you as you have been with me,". He knew I was right. He was looking for a response; or better- an answer.

I watched him cast his eyes away in shame. He didn't know I and shame went way back. I knew just how to deal with her. "So, if I didn't say anything about your sexuality or relationship habits, why did you choose to bring them up?" I asked him as if I really didn't know. He sighed, almost in relief.

"My birthday is next week." He announced.

"Ayyye! TURN UP FOR YOUR BIRTHDAY! Yuhh!!" I shouted as if we weren't in public. "What's the plans?" I asked hoping to lift is spirits a bit.

"See! That's the F*#*ing problem!" he had gone from zero to ten rather rapidly, forcing me to take a step back and give him my, 'Try Jesus, Not Me' face so he knew what it was and would have ample opportunity to lower his tone if he wanted to continue speaking with me.

It worked. He took a deep breath and spoke, "I brought it up because I did have plans- not for my birthday- but for like, life. I am attracted to guys and always have been… I think. But deep down, I did always think I was going to be married and have a family, too. I wanted to be a better dad than mine ever was to me. If I had kids, I would protect them. I just… I never got a chance because… well, I thought I was doing the right thing. I wasn't good with girls and there was a guy- the one I told you about, who saw me. He really saw me for who I was, and he liked me. I didn't have to embarrass myself chasing him. It felt good to be wanted…. desired," he defended.

"Of course it does," I acknowledged. I could not help but think back to the first time I realized God truly desired me. He wanted a relationship with me- one that did not require any pretenses from me. and feelings as I let him continue.

"I liked a girl before, a few of them, actually. But they were out of my league. There was this one girl, I really thought we had something... but the relationship didn't work out. I guess she really was never that into me at all. She was just using me. It just made me angry."

"Hmmm. It sounds like you have been hurt. Old girl really messed with your emotions. I am so sorry you had to experience that. I can also understand being young and needing love and all you get is rejection and misunderstood. Why wouldn't you give yourself to someone who finally took the time to at least try to make you feel valuable. Why wouldn't you do what finally felt easy after all the hard stuff?" I hit him with the #ActiveListening. He felt relieved and safe enough to continue.

"You asked why I brought up being gay," he reminded me. I hadn't forgotten.

"Yeah."

"I brought it up because I turn 30 next week. I'm not young anymore. I really wanted to have kids. A wife who loves me for me. The last woman who loved me was my grandma. I can never forget that. She was like a mom to me, and I wanted my kids to have that. I don't have a family. I don't have anyone to share everything I am with or anyone to pass all my smarts to. Everything good I do, everything I'm doing better than my dad did stops with me. I don't know who I am going to celebrate my golden birthday with because- yeah, I have guy friends... but look what they did to me. I like them but they remind me that I am 30 and I am sick. Them and my parents remind me that I have to take a lot of pills every single day. They remind me that I can't afford to miss a doctor's appointment. They didn't have PrEP this accessible back when I started out,".

I continued listening in silence. "I think that's why I used to drink so much. I knew I couldn't marry any of them. I don't think I want to. What's the point? We can't really make anything together. Trust, you know I tried," we laughed at an inside joke he probably wouldn't want published in this book. "Even if me and the guy I told you about did make love- we we didn't have to be married to do that. We could have gotten married, but I don't think he wanted to. I don't think I did either. I don't even think he really loved me."

We sat in silence a long while after that. Given the nature of our relationship, there were limits on what I could say. So, I let the Holy Spirit finish up the rest of the conversation before I let him know that as long as he had life, he had hope, and it was never too late to do what he believed would improve the quality of his life and help him reach his goals. I made sure he knew he was loved and cared for and that he deserved all the best things in life, including an eternal one.

Millennials and Gen Z's Be Like...

I titled the preface, "Math". I hated math until I came up with a dope definition for it. "Now, hold on, Sis. You turned down scholarships... You didn't know the definition of engineering. But you feel qualified to make up your own definitions now?" If you asked this question in your heart, I am not offended. It's valid. But any philosopher or mathematician will tell you that no official definition for the term "mathematics" has ever been established, at least not to the taste of most linguists or field practitioners. So, for the sake of this book, let's go with my definition:

> *Mathematics: The study of the replicate-able relationships that are formed to take up or detract from physical space and the impact it will have on its environment.*

We allow ourselves to be attracted to many things and over time...whether it be consciously, or unconsciously, these relationships have the capacity to make or break us. I learned a little more about engineering and why folks in that field are paid more than case managers. They're more than just designers and operators. You need them if you plan to build something of great value- they count the costs and risks- they understand how things work together. They know without them, all stakeholders are at risk of losing money, time and lives. Whatever is being built is too valuable for trial and error, hence engineers keep stakeholders from committing financial, material and physical suicide.

I think I am of a generation that is hell-bent on unfinished business and premature endings- all because we decided feeling better is more important. We don't like to cultivate anything, talk less of reproducing ourselves. Statistics show we are having less babies. We get married just long enough to make an Instagram Story and wedding video. We want to travel and live our best life... not give life because it's too much and earth is ghetto, and we don't know these babies they want us to have. That is why I'm writing this letter to a suicidal generation.

We are afraid to be uncomfortable because it might lead to pain, and we saw what that did to our forefathers. The problems we are tired of trying to solve for might disappear, with our natural, self-soothing decision patterns, but so will we. It feels good to do what feels good, especially if we feel like we have been deprived of somethings. It feels good to rebel against the machine of older generations who lacked love, lived lies and chose the emotionless experience of religion over the love of God. They didn't help us[3].

We are making decisions on flesh, by flesh and the only thing our flesh knows how to do is feel something until it dies. We have normalized killing ourselves with feel goods: Molly. Alcohol, Unhealthy/ unproductive sexual lifestyles. And the list goes on. We have made it a cultural norm to become irrelevant in God's greater plan. Tell me, is it more important to feel good and be validated than it is for you to make your mark on the world or reproduce the greatness God has put inside of you?

I am tired of watching us die slowly, right along with our destinies. How exactly are we killing ourselves?

---

[3] Please note I am speaking generally about each generation- some of us got it right. Many forefathers got it right. This is for who it applies to. As my grandfather would say, if you can't say amen, just say ouch.

Well besides the obvious, people typically kill themselves like this:

1) Trying to meet standards that have nothing to do with them.

2) Trying to take shortcuts in major areas of life.

STANDARDS THAT HAVE NOTHING TO DO WITH US

> *Do not conform yourselves to the standards of this world, but let God transform you inwardly by a complete change of your mind. Then you will be able to know the will of God - what is good and is pleasing to him and is perfect.*
>
> ***Romans 12:2, GNTA***

I came out of the womb different. I walked differently. I spoke differently. I thought differently. I was perfectly okay with that (most of the time), until high school. In high school, I met this girl... let's call her Keisha. Keisha and I had absolutely nothing in common aside from being two unreasonably short Black girls in high school.

Sheri Asuoha

This Girl Named Keisha

Keisha was also different than your average 14-year old, but she made it look so good! She somehow made those girls you saw on The Basement and 106 & Park[4]... and on the world's first reality TV shows seem attainable.

"So, how many boyfriends have you had?" "Umm..." I had never.

"Girl, aren't you 14? By now you should have at least been with at least 14 guys. I've been with 20 guys. My boyfriend is 18. You're probably still a virgin, aren't you? Don't tell people if you are...You already look like a lame."

"Umm..." Sheri and Shame...

"Girl, do you shave your legs?... Have you seen my new lipstick? You like it? Don't you use anything besides Vaseline? You like my eyeshadow? You don't have any

---

[4] What teens used to watch (or sneak and watch if your parents were Christian and you were only a Christian on Sundays) in the 1990's- basically music video countdowns. Music videos are what existed before "visual albums".

cute clothes, that like... fit? You know you could put some weave in your hair..."

This was Keisha. I can't tell you how many times I went home, confused, putting Vaseline on my eyelids as if it was eyeshadow. I cut myself using my stepdad's razors trying to learn how to shave my legs. I spoke with my mother about the weave. "I can do my weave myself," I told her. We don't need to discuss how that turned out.

I will tell you, in short, following Kiesha's advisement eventually made me hate myself. It led to me engaging in self-injurious behaviors, it added to the already tense relationship between my mother and I, exposed me to human traffickers, and the list goes on, but we can talk more about that later.

Pre-K (Pre-Keisha)

Before I met Keisha, I had two friends, Kim and Stacy. One of them- Kim, I had been talking to about Jesus (I had given my life to Christ... again... the summer before high school). Kim did not go to church.

"I be seeing those crazy church songs on TV- 'My life is in You Lord... My soap is in you, Lord...'" Kim sang, mockingly. "There's better songs...." Me and Stacy tried to tell her.

"So," Kim inquired one Monday after I and Stacy told her how we spent our weekends (in church). "...People just wake up and go to church every Sunday? You really get dressed and go out for no reason?"

"Yes, it's actually cool," I informed her.

"It's a lot of reasons. It's cute boys in church, too" Stacey chimed in. She was obviously not as saved as I was.

"That is crazy!" Kim laughed. "The idea that there are church boys is crazy," Kim always talked about church seeming crazy, but she never stopped asking me about it. Something in her wanted to know more.

Post-K (Post-Keisha)

One day Kim said to me, "Keisha has you out here, ex-church girl."

"What do you mean by that?" I said a bit defensively.

"I'm just saying, you're clearly not a church girl anymore. You went from 'My soap is in you, Lord' to whatever

YWM[2]

Trina[5] was talking in that song where she was wearing nothing but diamonds on her #%&@$."

She wasn't wrong. By this time, I no longer lived in my mother's house. My mom had thrown away or kept all my clothes. I only had what I left home with the last night I was there. I had an "auntie" step in and buy me junior versions of what she wore to 30 and up club on Saturday nights. I could not breathe in those clothes. I initially took them because I didn't have anything else, and she and Shame had informed me that I had no taste. But over time, I stopped trying to cover up and became quite comfortable being uncomfortable. I was hanging around boys I had nothing in common with and no interest in and I was forcing myself to listen to music that had nothing to do with me or my destiny so that I could be like Keisha... who seemed like everyone else. I even ditched school once.

Who Are We Supposed to Be?

At some point we have to normalize becoming who we are called to be and not who someone else thinks we

---

[5] Trina was a female wrapper from the early 2000's whose music often bore explicit lyrics.

should be. This is not a message for Millennials and my Gen Z friends, alone (we got it from somewhere). Baby Boomers and beyond are wearing themselves out striving for what has nothing to do with them at all!

I don't know if social media makes it worse. I just know that there is a generation of people who have made entire life decisions trying to measure up to another man's standards. People started churches, not because they were called to pastor, but somewhere along the line, they forgot God called them to teach elementary school children. Some people have picked up their entire family and moved them from one coast to the other because that's where all the most progressive people live or where they think they can have a fancier life, or an easier one. People have married the wrong person. People have aborted their children. All of these things are done with the best of intentions and for very sensible, logical reasons.

I did what Keisha suggested because I sincerely thought, at 14, that I was behind in life, and these were the things I was supposed to be doing if I wanted to keep up with everyone else.

YWM²

People commit suicide for the same reason. In the moment, it seems like the most sensible, logical thing to do- especially if your standard is the standard of the world. The purpose of this chapter is to remind you that there is always a better standard, one that suits you more because it was set by Him who created you.

If you are grown and reading this, take a moment to take stock of your life. Who or what is driving your decisions? Why? What do you need to do to ensure you are conforming to God's standard and not the worlds?

If you are almost grown, and you are reading this book, sis- you don't need to match the girls we see on TV. Bro- you do not need to try to measure up with the other guys and what they are doing. None of us need to be keeping up with Kardashians. The Kardashians are struggling to keep up with themselves. What you need to do is what King David was talking about in Psalm 37:

Mark the perfect man and behold the upright: for the end of that man is peace.

Psalm 37:37

Trust me, where there is peace, nothing is missing. Nothing is broken and all is well. That is definitely the place you want to be. Don't get me wrong. Nobody is born just knowing how to do life. Figure out what life you want to live and look for people who have become who you desire to become. Pattern yourself after them. I'll say more about this later, but the summer before my freshman year of high school, I had an encounter with Christ, and I decided I wanted to be like Him. He was free. He saw the best in people. He knew who He was. He was not bothered by the opinions of others, and He had a purpose.

How Did I Get Here?

I wanted to be like John Mark, The Evangelist. I had made mistakes and always imagined people would write me off. But like John Mark, I would be a writer (He wrote the Gospel of Mark) and the very people who wrote me off would need me some day[6].

I wanted to write and see visions like John, the Beloved. I wanted to be Christ's beloved and have deep revelations (See the entire book of Revelations and John 1, 2, 3). I wanted to be so important to God that no one could hurt me even if they tried.

---

[6]Acts 16:36-41

YWM²

I wanted to teach. I had in mind I would be like Apostle Paul, passionately teaching through my writing. I wanted to be as wise as Deborah, chilling under a palm tree, telling people what "thus saith the Lord"[7]. Deborah was my she-ro- the standard I wanted to be amongst men.

How I went from those standards to *Keisha*, I will never understand. What I do know is when I met Keisha (the spirit of this world), I began to really to give attention to the ways of the world. The world told me I was not enough. The world told me that my hair was not enough and that my "body count" was not enough. It told me that the way I knew to dress and the priorities I had chosen to subscribe to when I gave my life to Christ were sub-standard.

That is one key to knowing you are following the wrong standard. You will always be reaching for more, feeling like you are missing something when sin is your standard. In fact, according to mathematics, sin, literally means "opposite, divided by and without".

---

[7] 5 Judges 4

It is impossible to feel complete in sin and outside of Christ. What standards are you following? What is guiding the decisions you make? What standards are you setting? You need to know the answers to these because if you make the decision to follow standards that have nothing to do with you, you will die. Maybe not immediately but conforming to this image of this world is nothing short of a slow suicide.

I had forgotten that Christ's life was the one I should pattern myself after. I wanted to be a Christian. Not a "Keishan". May you never find yourself living like a "Keishan" in Jesus' mighty name.

The Shortcut to Destiny... Wait, no. Death.

Can you not discern this new day of destiny breaking forth around you? The early signs of my purposes and plans are bursting forth. The budding vines of new life are now blooming everywhere...
Song of Songs 2:13a

When something good is about to take place, sometimes, you want to tell people about it. It feels good to share good news, right? Or maybe the nature of what is about to happen is so great that if you tell people, it will ruin the surprise. Or maybe you know some people will not be able to believe it until they see it, so you do your best to keep it under wraps until the appointed time.

You might dress for the occasion if that is what is called for. You will likely be excited enough to do your research and learn everything there is to know about what will soon take place. You will equip yourself and be ready when the time comes for you to enjoy what you have been anticipating for what seems like eternity.

Keep that same energy about your destiny. You were designed for something great, or you would not exist. I have a definition of destiny for you. I did look some stuff up in the dictionary, but I read the Bible, too. The entire book is designed to equip you for destiny, so it made sense I study there in order to craft you the perfect definition for this word. Ready? Destiny is your guaranteed opportunity to do and be great on earth. It's basically a customized action plan for the impact you were birthed to make on the earth.

If you know ahead of time that your life is designed for you to do something great and be something great, honestly every day should be a great day for you. The entire day is designed with little easter eggs and pop-up events crafted especially for your destiny training. If you have this understanding- your entire outlook on life should be that of the sun shining and birds chirping because you know something great is about to happen, even when its dark as night and no birds are in sight.

The rates of clinical depression in the United States of America alone are outstanding and globally, around 264 billion people experience depressive symptoms (World Health Organization, 2020)[8]. Imagine the uncounted numbers of undiagnosed individuals. Let me put on my clinical hat to inform you that depression is not sadness. When you are clinically depressed, you cannot eat as you would normally. You don't sleep normally. You are either restless or overwhelmingly exhausted. You cannot think clearly.

These people are zombies. They are literally the walking dead. They go to school and work, and they do the bare minimum because nothing really has purpose. They just don't want everyone to know they are zombies, wearing a mask, going through the motions (that's if they can). These people are really, really sick!

---

[8] https://www.who.int/news-room/fact-sheets/detail/depression

And by "these people" I mean me. I am these people. I became a zombie in childhood and masked it in adulthood, smiling like a goofy while I was literally dead on the inside.

I found out over time that clinical depression is caused by a distorted or destroyed sense of destiny. Any doctor or therapist will tell you that you don't end up with Major Depressive Disorder or any clinical mental health diagnosis because something happened to you. This includes PTSD. Psychological problems such as these are triggered because of your attitude and preparedness for the experiences. So someone can experience a natural disaster and be fine. Why? They were mentally prepared for it. Hope was on their side. Whatever the incident was, they had capacity and they were able to conquer it while someone else can go through less and they end up suffering from anxiety or depressive symptoms for years to come.

I really did not want to preach to you. I much prefer telling stories and giving you the "tea" ... and I will... shortly. But preaching and teaching the gospel is in my DNA so you will need to learn to deal with it. I am going to share some really important scriptures with you, and I will use a nice translation, so you digest these words as easily as possible. I need you to do me a favor. If you are in a position to do so, read these scriptures out loud. I will tell you why later as I tell you another story.

I pray that the light of God will illuminate the eyes of your imagination, flooding you with light, until you experience the full revelation of the hope of his calling—that is, the wealth of God's glorious inheritances that he finds in us, his holy ones!

Proverbs 16:4a

Through our union with Christ we too have been claimed by God as his own inheritance. Before we were even born, he gave us our destiny; that we would fulfill the plan of God who always accomplishes every purpose and plan in his heart.

Ephesians 1:11

We have become his poetry, a re-created people that will fulfill the destiny he has given each of us, for we are joined to Jesus, the Anointed One. Even before we were born, God planned in advance our destiny and the good works we would do to fulfill it!

Ephesians 2:10

Never doubt God's mighty power to work in you and accomplish all this. He will achieve infinitely more than your greatest request, your most unbelievable dream, and exceed your wildest imagination! He will outdo them all, for his miraculous power constantly energizes you.

Ephesians 3:20

...For the Lord has a hidden storehouse of wisdom made accessible to his godly ones. He becomes your personal bodyguard as you follow his ways, protecting and guarding you as you choose what is right. Then you will discover all that is

YWM²

just, proper, and fair, and be empowered to make the right decisions as you walk into your destiny. When wisdom wins your heart and revelation breaks in, true pleasure enters your soul.

Proverbs 2:7-10

It is the Lord who directs your life, for each step you take is ordained by God to bring you closer to your destiny. So much of your life, then, remains a mystery!

Proverbs 20:24

Having determined our destiny ahead of time, he called us to himself and transferred his perfect righteousness to everyone he called. And those who possess his perfect righteousness he co-glorified with his Son!

Romans 8:30

Get up and stand to your feet, for I have appeared to you to reveal your destiny and to commission you as my assistant. You will be a witness to what you have seen and to the things I will reveal whenever I appear to you. You are not forgotten, for you have been chosen and destined by Father God. The Holy Spirit has set you apart to be God's holy ones, obedient followers of Jesus Christ who have been gloriously sprinkled with his blood. May God's delightful grace and peace cascade over you many times over!

1 Peter 1:2

Night's darkness is dissolving away as a new day of destiny dawns. So we must once and for all strip away what is done in the shadows of darkness, removing it like filthy clothes. And once and for all we clothe ourselves with the radiance of light as our weapon.

Romans 13:12

Sheri Asuoha

Set your gaze on the path before you. With fixed purpose, looking straight ahead, ignore life's distractions.

Proverbs 4:25

Here is the thing. The devil has a habit of helping us decide that the wrong things are what is most important. I had you read all these scriptures because I need you to internalize the truth that your "making" or becoming matters so much to God and matters even more to the world. The entire world depends on you becoming all that God has destined you to be. No pressure.

It is important I share this because I can guarantee you, that even if you get as far as finally realizing that your life has purpose, he will make you think that as long as you obtain a certain status or acquire a certain amount of money, or a certain feeling or vibe that you are successful, and you have made it.

Today, our generation is literally killing themselves just trying to feel something and be something. Be it through drugs, ungodly relationships, or the pride of life, it is easy for us to think we have found a short cut to the good life. Even obsessively doing good works will not get you to where God wants you to be.

Write all the books, get a billion IG followers and you can still miss becoming who God wants you to be and end up almost killing yourself. I know because, on the outside, I was doing everything right while the devil enjoyed the show of my self-righteous suicide mission. I was killing myself trying to do the most, when all I needed to do was trust God's plan for my life and enjoy my journey.

HOW IT ALL ENDS

Years later, I ran into Keisha on social media. We greeted and checked in and talked about our kids. We both have three girls. Her girls are almost as pretty as mine (side-eye). We both live in comparable suburbs. She looks great. I told her how good she looked.

"Girl, thank you!" she replied. "You know how I do." I won't even lie. I was almost delivered from the spirit of Chik-Fil-A and cheeseburgers calculating the difference in our figures (My deliverance and overcoming of fast food came later).

"I need to get myself together. You make me wanna do a sit up!" I complimented.

"I gotta keep it how they like it." She bragged.

They? I thought to myself. *Okay.* I tried to dismiss what I thought I heard. Maybe she is single for whatever reason and dating.

"I settled down with a quickness to the glory of God, cuz' the dating scene is ratchet and only for the fierce of heart! At least for me. You know I was never any good at it. Are you seeing anyone? Any prospects?" I asked her, hoping I didn't sound too judgmental.

"Girl, I see a lot and they're all suspect! But they're all a'aight. I get what I get from each of them. I still talk to two of my girl's fathers… one of them is White. I got a couple of White guys, so you know I'm doing good. They all pay their child support so I'm not complaining. I gotta stay on the dark-skinned ones' daddy. But he's packing so… like I said, I get what I need," I almost choked on my chewing gum.

"I saw you have a husband!" she continued. "He's cute!"

"Thank you," I blushed. "I do what I can." He is handsome.

"So, which of your girl's father is he?" she asked.

What the ... forgive me, Father. I didn't know what to type for about two minutes. It struck me in that moment just how different we were, and I had to take another three minutes to give God the glory for His redeeming grace and for keeping me even in my hot girl days when I had absolutely no intentions of being kept. I took a deep breathe.

"He's all their father's. The only other Father they have is our Heavenly Father. Girl, it was so good talking to you! Did you have any prayer requests?" That's how that conversation ended. I pray that last conversation we had is not reflective of the rest of her life.

When I first wrote this chapter and showed it to my pastor, I left the last conversation I had with Keisha out. After he read it, he was like, "Great. But I expected you to talk about your outcomes. What happened to Keisha? What happened to you? What were the outcomes of your past decisions?"

Well, by the time I really reflected on my outcomes and all the things I did ... and how my kids might read this book someday... I personally did not feel that all the sharing of outcomes was necessary, but hey, if it saves a life...

You see what happened with Keisha. As for me, things all started out fairly well after I left home at 16... after almost being kidnapped, trafficked... again, etc. Everything turned around when I got myself into college. I was having Bible studies in my dorm room. I was ordained a peer minister. I was in the gospel choir making a joyful noise... a resident assistant. I was known for evangelizing on campus and everything. Then, shortly after Facebook came out, I became known for other stuff. Apparently, I hadn't gotten all the Keisha out yet.

Let me tell you about the time a got so drunk in college- it's actually quicker to tell you about the times I was sober. I used that time to buy drinks. One time, my room mates looked for me after a kickback for hours. When they finally found me, I was outside. On the ground. In the snow... with half one earring, one shoe and half a Baby Phat coat. Don't even ask me to explain that.

...Oh, and I learned that when you use your body or anything God has given you for purposes outside of His plan for it... you will definitely experience one or all of the following:

YWM²

- Mental and/or emotion instability
- Co-dependency and /or addiction.
- Brokenness and/or emptiness (not the 'life-poured-out-for-Jesus' kind)

I had to fight all of those for YEARS as a resultant effect of my decisions to cut corners and live a life that had nothing to do with me. I struggled with suicidal ideations for longer than I care to admit.

The only difference between Keisha and I, in the end, was our decision. There are no short cuts when you are on a great journey. Everything on the path is designed to prosper you and make more of you so God's Kingdom will increase on the earth. You cannot afford to skip any steps just like you cannot afford to stay in one place forever. Take time to know the One who has sent you on this great journey. Let Him guide you and make you and comfort you when it gets hard, and you will do well. And you will increase. Honestly, anything else will literally kill you.

{2}

The Art of the Cry

*The eyes of the Lord are on the righteous,
and his ears are attentive to their cry*
Psalm 34:15

I was talking to a girlfriend, years ago at my place and she started crying very suddenly. We were chilling one minute, talking about my new couch. Next thing I know, she was crying on it. She said she felt like God had broken His promise to her. She said He knew how important "it" was to her and He just didn't make it a priority.

"That really hurt me," she cried. "I'm doing all this stuff for Him and the church ... helping His children and representing Him and He just gone do me like that?" I was this close to agreeing with her and calling him out of his name as any loyal friend should until I remembered we were talking about my Lord and Savior, not her ex.

Still, I knew she was hurting, deeply. In fact, this kind of pain was deeper and more deadly than any form of ex or baby daddy drama.

"I feel you, but you know He has His reasons, right? He has been way too faithful for you not to trust His plans or at the very least, seek His face to know what's up. We could pray together." I suggested.

"Thanks, I'm good. I'm just going to keep my distance from Him for a while. Just until I get over it and so I don't get my hopes up like that ever again," If she didn't have hope, she couldn't have faith and without faith... [9]

I was shocked. She had always been so driven for Jesus. It said so on her bumper sticker. *Let me try a different approach,* I thought. "Remember, that time you met that guy at that conference? The two of you went out for coffee and you felt like you were really hitting it off..."

"Yeah, what about it?"

---

[9] Check out my book written with Pastor Dele Osunmakinde titled, "Faith Classic" for an interactive break down on the power of faith. Also Hebrews 11:8.

"You texted me, 'I have found my Boaz'. Twelve minutes later you texted back, 'Never mind. His hair line is NOT his own'. You said you couldn't stop staring at it and you didn't think it was going to work because if his hairline wasn't real, the whole relationship might turn out to be a lie. Then, I reminded you your eyelashes weren't yours either and you said, 'true' and decided to give him the benefit of the doubt, but then he never called you back- probably because of how you were staring at his head- I've never known you to be discrete…"

"His fake hairline was not discrete either. What's your point?" she whined, tears rolling silently down her cheek… snotty tissue all over my new couch.

"You said and I quote, 'he didn't qualify to have the audacity' to ghost you. But you and your lashes have the audacity to treat God like He is some random you met at a convention and can do without? You need Jesus almost as much as I do. How does moving farther away from Him help you understand Him better? Make it make sense, friend," Friend wasn't hearing me, though.

YWM²

Tears

I know how it feels when you've only ever experienced the power and awesomeness of God. Jesus knows that feeling well, too. He is everything to you and in you, until suddenly, and unexpectedly, it seems you have to fend for yourself.

When we are new Christians and we read in the scriptures of our covenant with The Most High, we see the rainbows, the mercy and treasures that transcend generations. We Christians love to bask in the goodies of God and eat from the hand of God. We will deliberately overlook the justice and judgment of our Covenant-Keeping King. We forget about His sovereignty and omniscience outside of praise and worship time. We expect Him to do what He promised, but we forget it takes two to tango. We are expected to have some *skin* in the game, too[10]. We have to be all in, else, it's not covenant.

---

[10] I was this close to typing ...*(fore)skin in the game*... as in circumcision, but because of the children... I'll save it for my next book, *Pure*. Be on the lookout.

Sheri Asuoha

What He Did Not Do

Back to my friend's tears. As my friend poured out her heart to me concerning her not so pleasant experience with God, recounting all that He did not do, I was reminded of something I learned in the book of Jeremiah, the weeping prophet. I let her cry her heart out. Then, when my friend was finally in a place to hear me, I got the Lysol© wipes and handled that situation, discreetly and tastefully. But, immediately after that, I gently informed her that God had not broken His promise to her.

"What do you mean? I am telling you; He didn't come through!" she cried through tears, mucous and about half an eyelash. "Sis, He didn't lie, Friend. He doesn't lie. He literally is the Truth and before this little situation, you knew Him as a promise and covenant keeping God. He can't just change up on you. He's not like us."

"But I heard Him! He promised me ABC. He said if I XYZ... He was gonna definitely ABC by the end of the year. It's a whole new year and it hit me the other day. God never did what He told me He was gone do," she whined.

"Friend, nowhere in this story have you told me that you XYZ'd. Did you do XYZ exactly like He told you?" "Yes! I mean more than usual... I tried but He already knew that was going to be a lot to ask of me..."

"So, basically, you didn't do what you agreed to do, but you're mad at Him because He invoked the consequences of a breached contract just like He said He would? How do you think covenant works, sis?"

I was low-key judging her, but I was high-key taking inventory of myself. I scored very low on the scale of faithfulness compared to how faithful God was towards me. While you may be judging me, where on the scale of faithfulness are you?

The Tale of the Weeping Prophet

Jeremiah and the rest of the crew of Judah taught me the value of covenant. Let's read about it together:

> *Then all the army officers, including Johanan son of Kareah and Jezaniah, son of Hoshaiah, and all the people from the least to the greatest approached 2 Jeremiah the prophet and said to him, "Please hear our petition and pray to the Lord your God for this entire remnant. For as you now see, though we were once many, now only a few are left. 3 Pray that the Lord your God will tell us where we should go and what we should do."*

"I have heard you," replied Jeremiah the prophet. "I will certainly pray to the Lord your God as you have requested; I will tell you everything the Lord says and will keep nothing back from you."

Then they said to Jeremiah, "May the Lord be a true and faithful witness against us if we do not act in accordance with everything the Lord, your God sends you to tell us. 6 Whether it is favorable or unfavorable, we will obey the Lord our God, to whom we are sending you, so that it will go well with us, for we will obey the Lord our God."

7 Ten days later the word of the Lord came to Jeremiah. 8 So he called together Johanan son of Kareah and all the army officers who were with him and all the people from the least to the greatest. 9 He said to them, "This is what the Lord, the God of Israel, to whom you sent me to present your petition, says: 10 'If you stay in this land, I will build you up and not tear you down; I will plant you and not uproot you, for I have relented concerning the disaster I have inflicted on you. 11 Do not be afraid of the king of Babylon, whom you now fear. Do not be afraid of him, declares the Lord, for I am with you and will save you and deliver you from his hands. 12 I will show you compassion so that he will have compassion on you and restore you to your land.'

13 "However, if you say, 'We will not stay in this land,' and so disobey the Lord your God, 14 and if you say, 'No, we will go and live in Egypt, where we will not see war or hear the trumpet or be hungry for bread,' 15 then hear the word of the Lord, you remnant of Judah. This is what the Lord, Almighty, the God of Israel, says: 'If you are determined to go to Egypt and you do go to settle there, 16 then the sword you fear will overtake you there, and the famine you dread will follow you into Egypt, and there you will die. 17 Indeed, all who are determined to go to Egypt to settle there will die by the sword, famine and plague; not one of them will survive or escape the disaster I will bring on them.' 18 This is what the Lord, Almighty, the God of Israel, says: 'As my anger and wrath have been poured out on those

> *who lived in Jerusalem so will my wrath be poured out on you when you go to Egypt. You will be a curse and an object of horror, a curse and an object of reproach; you will never see this place again.' 19 "Remnant of Judah, the Lord has told you, 'Do not go to Egypt.' Be sure of this: I warn you today 20 that you made a fatal mistake when you sent me to the Lord your God and said, 'Pray to the Lord our God for us; tell us everything he says and we will do it.' 21 I have told you today, but you still have not obeyed the Lord your God in all he sent me to tell you. 22 So now, be sure of this: You will die by the sword, famine and plague in the place where you want to go to settle."*

God's chosen people broke covenant. Period. They saw Jeremiah's prophecy being fulfilled. They saw God's faithfulness. They breached their contract with God by telling Jeremiah that whatever God said to do, they would obey yet they did the total opposite (Jeremiah 42). God said, "Submit to the Babylonians and your lives will be spared,". They didn't have the faith to believe that God would protect them despite the evidence of God's faithfulness in Jeremiah's life right in front of them. What struck me was that they preferred to put their trust in the Egyptians- in the ones who enslaved them back in the day.

Isn't that just like us? Putting our trust in those overtime hours we claimed we were tired of, those humans that consistently let us down, etc.- then we want to cry about it.

Sheri Asuoha

Struggle Behavior

My initial thought concerning this: *Man, these Israelites were trifling! God is better than me because I don't have time for their level of disrespect and ingratitude. They mess up, then they cry, and He rescues them. Typical Israelite, struggle behavior.* Israelites, to me were not people of the Promise. They were people of problems. Everything about their story that I read wreaked of problematic behavior.

God reminded me that I had a drinking problem. He reminded me of my getting into all the wrong relationships problem, my body image problem... procrastination problem, petty social media posting problem, etc. All these were problems because He kept delivering me from them, but when I found myself in a tough spot, or life got too stressful for me, I went immediately back to all the devils I knew, instead of trusting God to make a way for me. Then, grown as I was, I would sit in the dark, or hide in the bathroom in the middle of the night, and I would cry about it.

All God wanted from the Jews was faithfulness in exchange for deliverance and a boatload of blessings unimaginable, but they could not be faithful. They could not keep covenant just like many of us can't today, steady backsliding and afraid of commitment.

The Ghetto of Unfairness

That's not even the deepest part of that story. The deepest part is about Jeremiah, the Weeping Prophet, himself. As far as I was concerned, His life was, what I can best describe as undeservingly unfair. It was very ghetto[11]. He was a prophetic bearer of bad news, and nobody really liked him, but they listened to him anyway and they were always going to him for information and advice. He was the Twitter of his time.

He was incarcerated & beaten[12]. His scribe and closest confident, Barry went through a terrible phase of selfishness at a time when Jeremiah needed him most (God had to get involved, it was so bad. Keep in mind his scribe is responsible for the words in the Book of Jeremiah we read today. A Kingdom scribe who cannot be trusted is dangerous to the world. If you are a scribe or sermon note taker in your church, or a writer or editor

---

[10]We use this term because of its real definition and origin, with respect to Jeremiah's Jewish heritage and the ironical context of the story. It has nothing to do with Black people.
[12]Jeremiah 37:15

for pastors and prophets and apostles like me, study the story of Baruch)[13]. As if Jeremiah's life was not chaotic enough, he sacrificed the little peace & blessing he could have enjoyed in Babylon (he had favor with them) in order to stay with and advocate for people who would not listen[14].

In fact, because the people were so adamant about sin, they forced him to go with them to Egypt, a place that he knew was going to be conquered and destroyed. I guess they thought God would not destroy the place as long as Jeremiah was with them there. That's the last we hear of Jeremiah. I mean, did he die? Did God rescue him? There's no clear-cut history of the outcome of his life. All we know is that he spent his whole young adult life crying.

Now, if Jeremiah's life does not seem "ghetto" enough to you yet imagine- God literally made Jeremiah buy one. That's right. God made him spend the little, hard earned money he had to invest in ratchet real estate. He bought an actual ghetto in Judah- land no one wanted[15].

---

[13] Jeremiah 45:4-5
[14] Jeremiah 40:4-6
[15] Jeremiah 38:8

YWM²

What Are You Crying for?

I encourage you to read Jeremiah's full story in his book of the bible. As you have read so far, the man had something to cry about. But He did not cry about his ratchet life. He cried the cry of a shepherd. He cried a very selfless cry. He cried because somebody needed to do it.

John the Baptist did the same thing. Jesus wept, too. None of the men I just mentioned cried because their lives were in shams (and trust me, they all went through some shady, unfair, sad situations in life.) None of them cried for themselves. They cried for others. They cried for the Kingdom of God to reign where sin and faithlessness were taking out more lives than failed police reform. None of those guys cried for themselves because they were clear about who they were. They knew their purpose, so they were able to cry for a greater cause- the salvation of Israel. The coming of God's glorious kingdom. What do you cry for?

Cry

This chapter is supposed to be a book. It will be soon in Jesus mighty name. Let me explain where I got the title from. When I was about seven, I was living with my mother and stepfather. This is significant to say because I did not get to live with them from the beginning and I was still adjusting to the culture.

One day my mother was going to the laundromat and apparently it was fun for us to go with her. I recall my (at the time) two other siblings wanting to go as well and crying hysterically when we could not tag along because we were taking too much time to get ready. My siblings were balling because we couldn't go. Especially, my crybaby little sister.

At that time, I wanted to be a chemist. I had plans to make a concoction that would either save the world or change the finish on my new dresser (It did the latter). Those plans were interrupted by my stepdad.

"Your mom left," He stated.

"Yes Sir," I responded.

"Aren't you sad about that?"

"Yes Sir," I responded. I wasn't. He paused, a bit, perhaps thinking about how to approach the subject with me in a way I would understand. "When people are sad, they cry.

YWM²

Don't you hear your sister crying?" Shorty was always crying, I thought to myself. A crybaby is going to do what a crybaby is going to do. She needs to learn that life is what it is. "Yes Sir," I responded, instead. "So, right now, you are sad. You don't like what is happening. So cry." He stood there waiting for me to cry.

The hell? I thought to myself. I learned how to curse earlier that year. Before then, I lived with my grandparents and there was no cursing in the house, but my new stepdad introduced me to a whole new world of words and in this moment, I applied one. Not out loud. I did not want to die. But in my head, I was like, ...*the hell is he talking about? Am I sincerely in trouble for not crying right now?! The hell...*

"I am not playing," he continued while I was still overusing the curse word in my head. "You will get no snacks and you will sit right here until you cry," I did not cry. I simply stole some snacks later and let my crybaby sister take the blame for it.

I remember meeting my stepdad, I think in Germany when I was three years old. I recall not getting my way about some Cheerios. I cried like I never cried before. I missed my grandmother. She cooked. What the hell were Cheerios? I remember crying relentlessly in hopes of things going back of normal and getting my very first spanking by him with my mother standing right there. I threw those Cheerios everywhere. At that time, I hardly knew either of them, but I learned from that terrible spanking- one I still remember to this day, "Shut your mouth, stop crying". From that time until well until adulthood- I did not cry.

This story is significant because a lot was going on in my family at the time. Then, I did not know why my stepfather was so stressed about my Mom going somewhere without us- but let's just say he had his reasons.

I remember little things would happen over the years; with my siblings- one time I saw a closet door fall on my sister, the same sister I said cried too much. And I just stood there. My mother asked me later, why I saw it and did not say anything, or try to help. It was the same reason I did not cry.

My Cry Baby Sister

At 7, I hated my life. None of it made sense. I was being forced to live in a world that I did not think I belonged to. I was not mean, but I lost all sense of care because my world was not what I desired it to be. I did not do it on purpose, but somehow, my pre-salvation life was one of apathy, selfishness and just getting through the day without getting in trouble with these people who I never genuinely formed a connection to.

Let me tell you about that crybaby little sister of mine. I'd never seen anything like her. I wasn't around when she was born so I knew nothing about babies or any other kind of human crying. Just crying. She cried when she could not go to the laundromat. She cried when she could not get the chips she wanted. She cried when she could not go outside. She cried (and fought) when my younger brother was being bullied in school and she did not like how my parents handled it. She cried and acted a whole fool when my mother put me out at 14... and at 16 or whenever I did not live with them.

She is in her thirties now and she still cries for every member of my family. She travails when things are not going as they should. My crybaby sister is now one of my closest confidants because she has a sincere heart for reconciliation and for crying out when things are not in order.

Your tears have power. Your voice has power. I know from experience that the devil does not want you to know that. He literally wants you to be in your feelings, controlled by them or completely dismissive of them. But your feelings are a weapon of mass destruction. Your tears have the power to change God's mind. How many times did the Israelites rebel against God? How many times did the cry out unto the Lord for mercy and healing and rescue? How many times God hear their cry and come to their rescue?

The art of the cry is simply to do it and to do it with a pure heart (the right motives and with purpose and with authority). When you surrender your life to Christ, you get His heart in exchange and the Holy Spirit pricks it in all the right ways so that your cry becomes a force to be reckoned with in the spirit world which makes all difference in changing things in this natural world that we live in.

A time came in adulthood when I started crying about everything, in the dark, in my bathroom. To my husband. To my pastors. You might say sweetheart, that sounds like clinical depression. Maybe. But if you understood what it was like to have all the feelings in the world until you literally had none- if you knew how it felt living for years without the capacity to cry out even when I was in danger or pain, you would better understand that those cornball tears of mine were a sign that deliverance was on the way.

Like my stepfather said that time when I was 7, when things are not right, you should cry. At the time in those laundromat days of my life, my family was on fire. Literally, there was a fire, but we will save that story for another day. The Lord actually began to give me dreams about the things that were going on. When I chose apathy, he gave that anointing for prophetic dream to my youngest sister- not the cry baby- but my youngest younger sister. We call her, *The Dreamer*. She was born after the laundromat situation. The point is the devil knew my destiny better than I did. He knew all my sibling's destiny's as well. So he willed to make me apathetic, make my crybaby sister dramatic, make my dreamer sister -and my younger brother- God's anointed as carnal and as detached from the things of the spirit as possible.

We all would have the voice and tears- the voice and tears with the power to get our family back in order and to be an example for this generation, generations to come and even the generations before us. We were created as a force to be reckoned with. But we only needed to master the art of the cry. What have you learned to cry for?

Destiny Cry

Me crying in the secret as an adult was actually a response to my frustrated destiny. I will tell you more about that later, but right now, please learn what I learned from Jeremiah. He could endure the way he did only because he held on to what God told him about himself. He not only held on to the precious promises of God for His life:

> [11] *For I know the plans I have for you," declares the LORD, "plans to prosper you and not to harm you, plans to give you hope and a future.*
>
> **Jeremiah 29:11**

He held on firmly to the instructions God gave Him for His life:

> *The word of the Lord came to me, saying, 5 "Before I formed you in the womb I knew you, before you were born, I set you **apart**; I appointed you as a prophet to the nations." 6 "Alas, Sovereign Lord," I said, "I do not know how to speak; I am too young." 7 But the Lord said to me, "Do not say, 'I am too young.' You must go to everyone I send you to and say whatever I command you. 8 Do not be afraid of them, for I am with you and will rescue you," declares the Lord. 9 Then the Lord*

> *reached out his hand and touched my mouth and said to me, "I have put my words in your mouth. 10 See, today I appoint you over nations and kingdoms to uproot and tear down, to destroy and overthrow, to build and to plant."*

As soon as you can understand that your life really is not about you, then you won't blame your family situation or life being unfair for the reasons you are crying... or in my case, not crying at all.

My friend- the one I started the chapter talking about has yet to understand that. But I pray one day, soon, she will. God has a plan for your life that is bigger than you. The sooner you find that out and subscribe to it, the sooner you'll have a good reason to cry. So, I'll ask you again. What are you crying for?

WHAT ARE YOU CRYING FOR?

At the dawn of Great and Terrible things there will be two cries:
The sorrows of
Men who forsake the expedient
And take refuge in reverie,
The men who are asleep in the time of warfare
And they who covet the countenance of strongmen
Will weep with the weak and wicked
Their mourning will echo amidst the smoldering and the Terrible
But there is the sound of a greater cry
The cry of men
Who do not slumber in the time of warfare
And in the dawn of Great and Terrible things
You will hear them travailing relentlessly
For the salvation of the brethren
This is the cry of the valiant
Warring for righteousness In the midst of famine,
Fearless in foreign lands,
And unmoved by the gods of this age
They are the voice of truth in a valley of lies
The valiant make victory the inheritance of
Their children
Boldly, they chant the anthem of the Kingdom
And in the time of Great and Terrible things
They will witness the greatness of their God and rejoice
For blessed and most favored are the valiant in Christ
Because they do not slumber in the time of war

- Sheri Asuoha

{3}

How Not to Drown in Troubled Waters

...If the Lord had not been on our side when people attacked us, they would have swallowed us alive when their anger flared against us; the flood would have engulfed us, the torrent would have swept over us, the raging waters would have swept us away.

Psalm 124:2-5

When I very young, I went to the beach with my mother and some church members. It felt like the most fun and freedom I ever had. The church members were doing their own thing, which left me to my own devices. I did not care much for the sand. I only enjoyed looking at the water. I enjoyed the opportunity to feel free and independent. I am not sure why I left the other kids, but something lured me to sit on the dock.

There was a lifeguard there. In those days, there were a few shows out such as Baywatch that depicted lifeguards as the coolest of the cool. I needed this cool teenage lifeguard that sat before me to know that at 8 or 9 years old, I, too was cool. I could wear a swimsuit and sit majestically over the water watching everybody and everything. The lifeguard smiled at me as I sat, her legs gently kicking in the beach breeze. I can kick my legs in the gentle beach breeze, too. When I realized she was not paying me or my breeze kicking legs any attention, I proceeded to mind my own business as well.

Bay Watch

I gazed at the dark water. I wish I could tell you it was clear blue and sparkling, but it was Lake Michigan. I wanted to see if I could see any fish or hidden treasure in the dark, foggy water. I wanted to see if I could kick my legs until they grew longer. I tried to do both things at the same time until I finally fell in. That's when I recognized that the major difference between me and the very cool, long- legged teenage lifeguard is that she could swim. I could not.

"Help! Please!" The weight of the water overpowered my cry for help. I can still taste it. I looked up at the long-legged lifeguard, but I could hardly see her clearly with all of Lake Michigan gauging at my eyes. Did she see me? Did she care to save me? She did not move. Where was my mom?

"Help, Mommy!" Help was not coming. So I decided it was time I learn to swim. You know, while I was drowning. I swung my limbs frantically. I tried to do everything I saw on Baywatch. The more I tried to save myself, the more the waters overpowered me until I fully surrendered.

The next thing I saw after darkness and the end, was the sky. Once I accepted that it is not when I am sinking that I can teach myself to swim, the long-legged lifeguard was able to jump in and rescue me.

I drowned a few more times after that. I drowned in toxic, unhealthy relationships. I drowned in deep depression and bitterness. Anxiety and alcoholism. Here is what I learned from every one of my drowning experiences: you cannot rescue yourself. There is a very necessary component of surrender and accepted vulnerability needed for a seasoned source to come and rescue you.

Sheri Asuoha

Learning to Swim

This chapter is about how to keep yourself from drowning. If you do find yourself drowning, it is about how to make a comeback. The most wasteful, dangerous (and foolish) thing you can ever do is almost lose something- something of high value- your gift, your anointing, your life, your salvation, etc.- and you learn nothing from it. Learn. I don't just mean make deep thoughts about how you will do better next time. True learning is indicated by a change in behavior.

There was a Judean king, King Manasseh. Like me at age 8, he wanted to swing his legs a bit. He became king at age 12 and it seems he, too was highly influenced by what was around him. He began to emulate other kingdoms- wicked ones, doing what was detestable in the Lord's sight until God had enough and was ready to punish him. Manasseh pushed his luck to the point of drowning. He was sinking in sin and the consequences thereof. But he did something we can learn from. He got new information that caused him to change his fatal behavior. He learned.

YWM²

The Tall Tale of Little King Manasseh

Let's use his life as a case study. I am going to give you key steps to take to make your comeback so that when you find yourself in troubled water, you don't drown.

> *10 The Lord spoke to Manasseh and his people, but they ignored all his warnings. ¹¹ So the Lord sent the commanders of the Assyrian armies, and they took Manasseh prisoner. They put a ring through his nose, bound him in bronze chains, and led him away to Babylon. ¹² But while in deep distress, Manasseh sought the Lord his God and sincerely humbled himself before the God of his ancestors. ¹³ And when he prayed, the Lord listened to him and was moved by his request. So the Lord brought Manasseh back to Jerusalem and to his kingdom. Then Manasseh finally realized that the Lord alone is God!*
>
> ***2 Chronicles 33:10-13***

1. Recognize you are drowning. You have to know when you are in troubled water. This seems simple enough, but by default, humans are flesh and therefore prone to pride. Do not be proud because that leads to denial...which leads to getting in over your head... which leads to drowning. Admit to yourself and to God that you are in a situation, and you need help. When King Manasseh realized he

was in chains, once a king, now bearing a slave's nose ring- he had to admit that he was in over his head and about to drown (2 Chronicles 33:11).

2. Repent sincerely. Once you recognize you are drowning, admit it. Tell God your bad and mean it. King Manasseh, as awful a king he was, repented. That's something many evil kings before him did not do and it made a difference. Remember King Saul? He lost the throne and drowned in depression, paranoia and other insanity because he had no remorse while King David did Uriah dirty, but genuinely repented and the scepter never left his lineage. Don't wait or assume God will just forgive you and have mercy, while His enduring mercy may give you time and a chance, you have to make a conscious decision to change through your genuine repentance. Saul, the one who became Paul eventually didn't just get converted because of his encounter with God. He changed because he was a repentant sinner. Learn from that.

3. Invoke the mercy of God. As I said earlier, it's not God's mercy alone that will bring you lasting salvation, but it is not repentance alone, either. You must duly seek for God's mercy. Intentionally

ask for it and apply it liberally. King Manasseh demonstrates what this looks like in 2 Chronicles 33:13 and we see the positive consequence.

4. Yield to God's program for your life. Once King Manasseh received God's mercy, he got back in line and did what God wanted him to do. You don't know what God wants you to do? What is the last thing He told you to do that you didn't do or didn't do very well? Do that thing. Don't know what that is? Ask Him. Can't hear Him? Start doing what is needed in God's vineyard. As you work for the Lord, cleaning the church or helping with the children or ushering and anything else you can lay your hands on, God will speak to you, but also it will keep you safely in God's will, so you don't find yourself kicking against the goads like I was that day when I was eight.

That Lying...

When you make a mistake, intentionally or not, it does not have to be the end. Don't let the devil slap you with guilt, condemnation or apathy. Don't let him push you to a place of total rebellion. Don't let him trick you into giving up. Sincerely yours, as long as there is life, there is hope. God wants to give you another chance.

Learn, truly learn from your error and follow the steps above to enjoy redemption.

Will there be consequences? Yes, silly. You messed up. But the mercy of God is far more potent than whatever your consequence will be. Enjoy both and make the devil look at himself in the mirror to see the liar he really is. All he ever wanted to do was get you out of the will of God so he can keep himself safe. Once you refuse to leave God's presence, he loses.

Having to take an alternate course on the path God designed for your life is not ideal. Let me stress that. But it is far better than totally missing out. Trust me I know. I can only imagine how great my life would be had I not believed the devil's lie that because of childhood pains or the unfair experiences that I endured. My life did not matter.

I made many reckless, flesh and pride driven decisions. But I had a lot of old friends who did the same things. The difference between me and them: I eventually acknowledged that I don't know how to swim. I cried out to God for help and mercy. He gave me instructions. I listened (even though they were really strange instructions- like having a Nigerian man's baby, etc.).

YWM²

Speaking of which, yes, God gave me my husband who helped me exponentially. He gave me my children to keep me structured and grounded. He gave me my pastors and slowly began to give me the right friends. I have allowed Him to guide my path since. It has made all the difference. I don't have to compare myself to anyone else, good or bad, now because I'm on a great journey tailor made for me. As long as I stay the course, I can't drown. I can't get into trouble. May you find your path, get there and stay there in Jesus' mighty name.

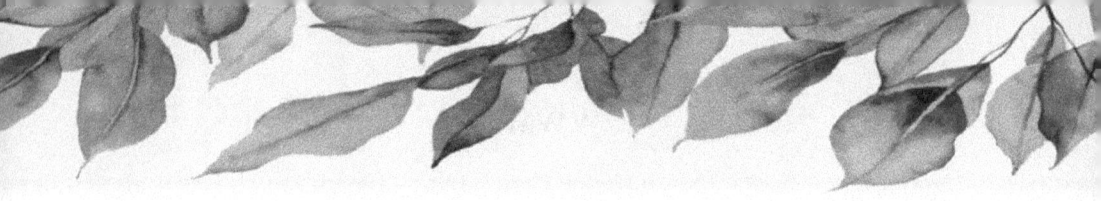

Troubled Waters

The time is coming
When the waters will rise...
The earth will shake
Breaking the strong holds
That our bones were too weak to shatter
The waters will rise
And stones will cry out in victory and injury alike
The plight of the sanguine will be revealed
And the infamously doubtful will be forced
To yield to Truth
The waters will rise
And spatter those who strove to
Appear white and unspoiled
They will bruise, envelope, and conquer
And there will be no time to prepare
And no mountain of retreat
But while they are still...
Let us be led to them
And let us find rest
While pastures are green
The time is coming and is now... Let Him lead you.

-Sherilynn Asuoha

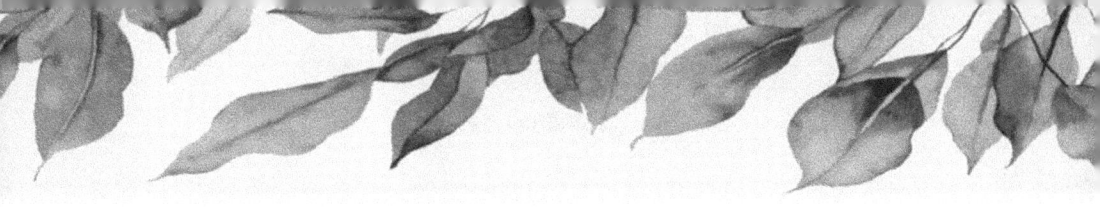

{4}

There's Nothing Wrong with You

...God look at her and said, "There is nothing wrong with you," and evening passed. And morning came.
Genesis 1:31, Sheri Translation

"Ms. Jones... Ms. Jones, guess what." I said with my stuffy, first grade nose. It was 1991 and I was a student in the Chicago Public School system. I imagine Ms. Jones had more important things to do than entertain my request for her attention. Nevertheless, she responded. "What is it, Sherilynn?"

"I learned how to gospel rap,"

"What?"

"You listen to rap, right? So I need you to know there's gospel rap. It's better than any other rap because it's about Jesus. I rap my own songs about Jesus, too. I started rapping when I was two years old. But I didn't write any raps yet except for one, but it's not finished[16]. But listen to this one I learned from my Mommy's radio," I got into proper rap form.

It's Time...To Make That Change.

I began to make the rhythm, then I belted it out. "Well, it's time to make that change. People of the world today are fading. All of us have our ups and down's. You better think about it, or you won't be around. Now what you need is a little bit of love sent by One from heaven up above..."

About that time, Ms. Fook, the principal walked up. "Well, what's going on here?" she asked, probably judging my teacher's classroom management skills. I decided to help my teacher out by answering the question for her.

"I'm teaching Ms. Jones about gospel rap. A lot of people don't know... but it's better than any other rap because

---

[16] If you must know, it went, "I'm Sheril T. in the place to be and I'm FRESH! That's the whole song.

it's about Jesus. Do you want to hear? Here it goes... Well, it's time to make that change..."

The two teachers looked at each other bursting with laughter. "Girl, this is the strangest child I have ever met," Ms. Jones looked back at me, "You want to tell me about 'Jesus rap'? Go get in line. What on earth is 'Jesus rap'?" They continued to murmur to one another as I walked ashamedly to the line with the other first graders staring at me and laughing. I heard the principal say, "She's real smart though but strange. Girl, her whole family is strange..."

More Change...

That wasn't the last time I was called strange. Fast forward four or five years. I was in suburban schools now. I had been in suburban school for kindergarten, then a new one in third grade, then back at the same one I was in before in fourth grade, now I attended a different one for fifth grade- but many of the kids from my kindergarten and fourth grade experiences were also in this school.

I was standing in the hallway, alone as usual, when I noticed three of the most popular girls in school were storming my way in a fury. I braced myself until finally, the most popular girl of all, Lauren was directly in my face. There was no COVID-19 back then. We knew nothing of personal space at that time.

"What the hell were you doing talking to my man?!"

"What man? We're in fifth grade, Lauren." I reminded her. She curled her fists and glared at me as if she knew I knew who she was talking about. I did.

"Oh, you mean Munchie. He is not anyone's man. He is 12 like the rest of us," He might have been 13. There was a rumor he failed a grade. "I was just helping him with his homework, so he didn't fail English. Again," She wasn't happy with my response. "I help all the guys with their homework." Not sure why I thought that would help. By now her best friend, Tina had made her way through the crowd to co-sign on her behalf and stomp my brains out. Tina was the biggest of us fifth grade girls and most of the boys, too.

"You talking about being smart again, huh? I thought we made it clear. Ashley is the smartest, not you!" Tina thundered. "We all saw you get kicked out of the smart people class because you're too stupid to bring your book to school... You don't even know your own name!"

"That's true... what is her real name?" kids murmured across the small crowd. Tina wasn't wrong. I found out Sherilynn or some version of that was the name of the victim in a horror movie when kids started mocking me in school. I also got tired of people calling me "country" and always pronouncing my name wrong. The second I found out teachers had to call you whatever you told them to, I told every teacher a different version of my name until college.

I first tried Lynn. Someone told me that was a white person's name, so I tried going by my middle name, Ti'ar, which I felt was Blacker. Apparently, it was too Black, and I'd never get a job. But once my mother told me the meaning, I went to school and boldly proclaimed, "Ti'ar is not 'ghetto'. It's French. It has an accent mark, not an unnecessary apostrophe. It princess because mother knew I was royalty," I also told them I grew up in Europe, and that Ti'ar was a very common name in Paris, France.[17]

"She's lying," announced my Haitian classmate who apparently spoke fluent French or some version of it. She told everyone my name did not mean 'princess' and that there was no way I'd ever been to France especially with how terribly I dressed. She told me my mother lied to me because she probably did not know how to spell Tiara.

First of all, no one told me there were Black people who spoke French. Years after the humiliation, of being exposed as a liar by Frenchie, I learned Ti'ar really did mean 'a princess' crown'. My mother had not lied to me. I hope Frenchie reads this book so I can burst her bubble.

I preserved Sheri, because my Grandmother called me that name sometimes and it was between us. But by college, that the only nickname I hadn't tried. I finally decided to start going by given name my junior year. It was time to grow up. I informed my friends who looked

---

[17] I did live in Europe briefly- I schooled in Wiesbaden, Germany for maybe a year while my mother was in the army.

at me and said no, we aren't calling you anything else. Sheri it stayed.

"You're average," Tina went on. "Just like the rest of us. And you still dress like a dyke!"

I hated when she called me that. I had corduroy uniform pants my mom bought me from a garage sale. I might have picked them out myself, not realizing they were boys pants. "We're gonna ask you one more time. Why were you talking to Munchie?" she threatened.

"Again, I was helping him with his English. The same English I keep repeating to you," By this time, Ashley had come along. She was the smartest girl in school, and she hated my guts.

Story Telling

"You are a liar," Ashley announced plainly. "Everybody knows it. Nobody likes you. We ignored you in kindergarten because you were weird. Now that you're back from whatever foster home you were, at and you are still a liar, and you are really strange. In fact, why did you tell us all those made up stories about your life? Your dad is rich and has mansions? We all know you have no father. Look at how nappy your hair is. Clearly, the Mexican cop isn't your father," everyone laughed.

First of all, my Father does have mansions. In heaven. I used to have dreams about mansions and family. Those were the stories I told. I liked telling those stories better than the ones my mom told me about how my dad went to get diapers and never came back. He fathered my half siblings their entire childhood. Maybe because they had lighter skin?

Every Monday, my peers would come to school with stories about their very cool weekend and stable family lives. What was I to say about my life? I was a latchkey kid. From 8-14 years old, I was responsible for the house and care of my siblings while my mom and stepfather were at work. They worked multiple shifts at a time. My siblings fought a lot and did not always listen. But that was not all bad. It made me responsible. I did not know at the time, but by 16, I would be living on my own so all I learned being their caregiver while my mom was gone most days and nights came in handy.

But I went through other things that I could not talk about, but also, I could not hide. When kids at school were talking about eating pizza, was I to tell them that I mistakenly forgot to clean the food from the sink after washing dishes, so I had to eat the garbage that was left in the sink over night? That's why I was not feeling to well. That's why I was always sick. Was I to tell them the reason I did not wear shorts in the summer was because while they went to water parks, I and my siblings received cold water showers to prep our skin for extension cord beatings... my legs and arms and back bore welts and stayed swollen.

In the very near future, I'd be able to tell them we finally got our first fancy new house with a garage. I would have to sleep in the garage with the garbage cans and the dog I was terrified of, but I survived. I would also be able to tell them of the time I got ice cream and donuts and room service after my first surgery. I had fractured bones in my hand that had been left untreated too long after being beaten to what I thought would be my death with a giant wooden plank when I was 13.

After that beating, I was left to lay alone in the cat's concrete room under the stairs- that cat's room. I was allergic to cats and this cat, King David, we called him, was always attacking me. Deep down I thought they bought the cat kept him even though I was allergic hoping I would die naturally. I was laid out on the concrete floor over scratchy, poop-filled kitty litter. My eyes were as red and swollen as the rest of my body because of the cat fir. I couldn't move. I did cry. And if you recall, during childhood I almost never cried.

When I went to school the following week, kids called me the "Nutty Professor"- a character from a movie whose whole body had swollen up from an experiment. I told them it was a bee sting. The gym teacher knew it was a lie and sent me to the nurse, who forced my parents' hand to take me to the emergency room. I got a metal plate put in my hand which was very cool. My stepdad made me agree to say I fell of my bike. My mom apologized and said if I wanted to tell the truth and be taken away to live with another family, she would not be mad. I smiled and told her it was okay. And that is when I started planning my suicide. I was never supposed to be born to begin with.

The Candy Game

There were many stories like that- most, I blocked out of my memory. But also there were some good things- in fact something good was always paired with the bad. There were weekends when I got a lot of candy. It was when I went to my biological father's mother's home-

Grandma's house. I used to stay with her whenever school was out. Grandma was old and not in the best health. She was nice and I believe she loved me very much, but she often sat in one spot, so she never knew what was happening in the rest of the house, I think.

My older cousin also lived there. He was in a gang, Gangster Disciples, GDK, but I did not know it at the time. I just thought he and his friends were cool and loved to wear matching clothes. I would have loved to talk to my peers at school about all the cool candy I got from him and his gang friends. But I could not. I earned the candy by dancing or doing whatever the friends wanted me to do. If you did not, you were in trouble, my cousin told me. If you just relaxed and blocked it all out, you got candy and compliments.

Not Strange, Just Different

I could not share that story at school. So yes, I made up lots of stories as a child about how I imagined life should be for me. But in that moment, I needed to respond to the girl who was in my face with her two friends.

"I am not strange. I am different." I responded to her. I was not clever enough to come up with that myself. It was a line from a poem I found one day cleaning up at home. One of the best things my mother ever did for me is finally let me have my own room. It was short lived, but as she was preparing the room for me, there were lots of old things she packed up that needed organizing. As I was going through those things, I found old yearbooks of my mother pregnant with me in high school and all the smart comments her peers of the time wrote about how terrible I would be (they were kid's joking, I'm sure. My mom was popular and mischievous in those days).

When you are as young and as impressionable as I was, you don't see comments like the things her friends said as funny. I thought it was my prophecy. I should have brought it up to her that I read the comments so she could have set me straight, but instead I internalized that everyone always knew I would be ugly, and stupid and bad, and ruin her life, etc.

But I found something else in all of her throwbacks that stuck with me more than her yearbook did. I found a poem- maybe the first poem I ever paid attention to. It was written by my uncle when he was a kid. It was titled, *Not Strange, Just Different*. He, too, had struggles growing up and fitting in and he wrote the poem based on what my grandmother would tell him about his life. I wish I could find the poem to share here, and my uncle gave me permission to rewrite it- which I did do about 20 years ago. But I couldn't do it justice. It was a poem of complaints- if you've ever read the book of Habakkuk, it's like that only it's my grandmother doing the replying- telling him not see himself as the world does but to live according to His prophecy. "You're not strange…" she would use to counter his negative self-talk. "You are Different".

I get on the kids nerves at church about how privileged they are to have teachers and mentors and pastors who genuinely love them and desire they take their life and destiny seriously. The closest thing to any of that for me was that poem. Talk about the miracle of sufficiency- that poem kept me long enough to finally meet people who help me (intentionally or not) on my great journey. I read that poem on repeat, unconsciously encouraging myself. Then I started writing poems. Then books. I decided I wanted to be a writer and for the first time, things started making sense. My mother, saw my interest in writing and encouraged it. She told me she wrote too and eventually invested heavily in making sure

I would have what it takes to be a writer- including buying me my first writing desk. It was white wicker. She bought all the matching furniture too desk- to date, that room she made for me was the safest space I can remember and the place I had all my most important dreams. She bought me a word processor (a hybrid between typewriter and computer) and she even let me stay with my uncle one summer to learn the art of writing.

Now that's the story I should have shared with my peers at school, but the devil was clever enough to let me forget all about that. Write your prophecies down. Write down the good things- your testimonies. I shared a lot in this chapter- the things Satan would love to let linger in my mind and heart. But my mother proofread this book. My biological Father- wasn't there when I was a kid- but he blesses my children every single year. Oh, and my rapist not only served time, but he also called me from jail to repent. The only thing lingering in my life is the fulfillment of prophecy and a bunch of testimonies.

Oreo

"You're definitely different," Tina retorted. "But you are not better than us. In fact, you ain't nothing but an Oreo- Black as ever on the outside, white on the inside." The crowd of students went wild. As far as they were concerned, there was about to be a fight. All this because I helped a boy write his English assignment.

Retrospectively, why were they so threatened? I thought I was a 'dyke', right, Tina? She gave me the nickname. Now I'm an Oreo. Okay.

I love Oreos, I thought to myself. *I don't like being called a dyke.* To this day, Oreos remain my favorite snack because they remind me of how God spared me from what could have been my demise. I had never been in a fight. And if it was anything like dancing, I could not do it. But something about Oreos put my mind at ease.

Angels & Oreos | Perfect Peace

Where I should have been afraid, all I felt was peace, perfected. I felt angels were with me. My mind was on angels and Oreos.

I looked Tina in the eyes, "You are an inside out Oreo," I caught them off guard with that reply. "I am dark on the outside and white inside. How? Because I speak English? I don't have any white people in my family. Not sure how there's white in me, but okay. My stepdad is Puerto Rican... he looks kind of white, but as you just let the world know, he is not my real dad. But you look very pale for a Black person. Inside out Oreo. White on the outside. Dark in the heart. That's your problem, not mine..." mic drop. Retrospectively, it was very corny. In fact, the crowd of kids didn't know how to respond. I had confused the enemy and put the crowd in a panic.

"Girl, what is wrong with you?!" That's all Tina could say before storming away. "Let's go!" she signaled to Lauren and Ashley and just like that, the crowd disbursed.

What's Wrong with Me?

What's wrong with you? I was asked that question many more times still.

Years later, in college, one of my favorite professors asked me the same thing. "What is wrong with you? Where is your head? You write these amazing papers, but your exam scores don't make sense. You are failing my class when I know you can do better. Are you even paying attention when you take your exams?" She mentioned some of my other erratic behaviors. I talked way too fast. I was never on task, I was never on time, easily distracted, daydreamed.

She referred me to a psychologist as a mandate if I wanted to move forward in my coursework and not fail. The psychologist did testing on me for about 3 months. She confirmed a diagnosis consistent with attention deficit disorder and mentioned some stuff about my mood and depression.

What is so wrong with me that as an adult, I was referred to a psychologist and a psychiatrist for issues children typically have? What was so wrong with me that my mother could not love me the way she loved my other siblings or the cat. Or the dog? Or everyone else's kids, literally, all over the world (she was a missionary). What is so wrong with me that my father me left- but stayed with his other kids throughout their childhood?

The Answer

One thing about Jesus... He is the answer. He gave me answers to all of my questions when I began to genuinely seek clarity. The first time He answered me was through my uncle's poem. I was not strange. He told me. My situation was strange. My life and destiny was just... different. He allowed me to go through different experiences- not because He did not care about me. He knew more about me than I did because He knew my future.

Ideally, there were things I should have never had to go through. But there were some battles that neither of my grandparents or parents had been able to fight much less win. But for the sake of generations that needed to come through me, someone had to fight and win.

Years later I would work with children who faced the unimaginable. The horror stories I shared can't be compared to what these children have gone through. When they acted out in rage because nobody understood them or believed them, for the sake of the glorious destinies they had ahead, God needed someone there who would understand very well and introduce them to the One who understood even better.

He needed someone to tell them there were angels fighting like mad on their behalf to keep them and their future alive. He needed someone who understood to tell them the devil is terrified of them and what they could soon do to his own tragic future. He needed someone who would be there who would tell them there was nothing wrong with them. He told me what was different about me in Deuteronomy 14:2:

> ² *You have been set apart as holy to the Lord your God, and he has chosen you from all the nations of the earth to be his own special treasure.*
>
> **Deuteronomy 14:2**

God gave me this image of a secret treasure buried deep in the ocean, one that survived a shipwreck. This treasure was so valuable that eventually someone was going to risk his life swimming deep to the bottom of the ocean just to find it and retrieve it even if it cost him everything. Whatever the person had to risk gaining that treasure, he would risk it because the treasure was worth much more.

The Answer II

I have one more story to share in this chapter before we round off. It was not until I was an adult that I really understood the answer to my question. This is also where I got the title for this particular chapter.

I was 25 and fully born again. I was ministering and leading... I was married with children when suddenly my life flew into a frenzy as I began to have strange, negative experiences that were not in line with what I understood to be a part of my salvation package.

I was following a man I had recently taken to be my spiritual father- something I never heard of before- I never really had a father and I decided that he was a simple guy with big dreams who was very clear about where he was going. He had the right idea about God. I was a Bible snob at the time- obsessed with God's word. Outside of Dr. Myles Monroe, I had not met anyone who really understood the Kingdom of God. He did, so I trusted him and told him everything in hopes he can help me stay on the right track and become everything I was meant to be in life. I truly believed my future was great.

The Cancer Problem

But I got sick. Some of the symptoms were very visible and I was sent home from work one day until I returned with a doctor's note. I went to the doctor and the doctor referred me to an oncologist. "What's wrong with me?" I asked the oncologist. He found something happening in my body and called some other physicians to look as well. They were concerned I had multiple myeloma- a type of cancer more typical in older people. They scheduled me for a bunch of tests.

I sent my father in Christ a message. I was pouring out my heart to him about everything that was wrong with me via chat. He sent me some "answers of peace". I went back for more blood draws at a cancer treatment center. I was the youngest one there it seemed. They gave me biohazard jugs to pee in for a week. I reread those "answers of peace" my father in destiny gave me and I prayed.

The day came when I was to return the biohazard jugs of refrigerated urine. They drew more blood. I saw sick, dying people all around me. I went into a small panic. I finally was living my best life. I was director in my workplace, the youngest in its history. I was obtaining my doctorate. I was finally *happily* married, with children- two things I thought I might never have and did not deserve. I was finally getting life right, and still. something was wrong with me. *I can't win*, I thought.

I texted my spiritual father again. Maybe he did not get the magnitude of what was going on in my life. Around that time I also started struggling at work in my new director role. I remembered the diagnosis I got in college. How on earth did I think I could lead an organization, obtain my doctorate? I had started an editing company with no experience. I was trying to raise children in spite of my horrible childhood and be a wife when I had never seen a healthy relationship. *What's wrong with you*, I asked myself again.

I got in my car and was driving home, still in disbelief that I was having this experience despite my covenant with God. I checked my phone before I drove off in hopes of more answers of peace. Nothing. Maybe my spiritual father finally figured out I was a lost cause. I thought about how it would be when I got the final news about my cancer case. As I was driving, my phone pinged. My spiritual father, soon to be pastor returned my message:

"OluwaSheri, there is nothing wrong with you," I had not told him that this was still a major thought in my heart. His sensitivity in responding that way made me pull my car over to carefully read he message.

There is nothing wrong with you. I read it again. Maybe he thought I was lying about the diagnosis. Maybe he did not know my mother almost died of cancer when she was fairly young. I remember how her body looked as if it was decaying, while she was lying in a hospital bed. I think she weighed less than 80 pounds. It was the first time I'd seen her since she put me out the house.

Maybe I needed to show him the paperwork and tests from the treatment center. Maybe I should have taken selfies while I was sitting in the waiting room with sad, scared, elderly people waiting to die. But I kept reading.

He went on to tell me who I was in Christ, and he reminded me of the covenants we always talked about. "You are not dying. You are not going to die..." he continued to say. Then he made me what we called a "concoction". He always spelled it wrong- he would spell 'concussion'. I never corrected him because the concoctions were so mind-blowing, the name was almost fitting. They were prayer points that I think gave the devil a concussion every time. I prayed them until my next appointment.

Sheri Asuoha

The Miracle

During the next appointment the doctors showed me everything that was wrong. They pointed out abnormalities with some system in my body, but they said something even more interesting was happening with my immune system- I kid you not they said the abnormality was like healing process they never saw before.

"It's best we let it keep doing what it's doing. Something was there, but its healing. It's. best to let it keep running its course," they said. I was confused.

"So, I'm... okay? There's nothing wrong with me?" I asked. "Whatever was wrong- and there was something wrong- your body is fighting it like crazy, that's why you broke out how you did. We just can't tell what it was because of how your body is healing. I guess you can thank God. It's a miracle," he looked at the other doctor who nodded in agreement. "Other than that, we notice your iron is dangerously low. We recommend an iron infusion; we can schedule you to come back for that," After the infusion, I never stepped in the cancer treatment center again.

YWM²

Jesus, the Lamb and Word of God, is perfect, and He is the answer. I am a witness to that. Once you accept Him as both Savior and Lord of your life, you have the

{5}
Learning to Walk

Arise, walk about the land through its length and breadth; for I will give it to you.
Genesis 13:17

My mother never let us go anywhere by ourselves. But she let me go somewhere once. Just once. She let me walk by myself to Greco candy store in Glenwood, Illinois. It was a big deal. Weeks earlier, I had given my life to Christ, again. I first decided to follow Jesus around age 7. Remember, shortly after that I started my gospel rap ministry.

But I was older now. My life had completely changed! For example, my mom knew I hated dogs. But after I gave my life to Christ, without being asked, and though it was not my chore, I started taking our dog, Samson, outside for his walks. I had read in 2 Timothy 1:7,

> *7 For God has not given us a spirit of fear, but of power and of love and of a sound mind.*
>
> **2 Timothy 2:7**

I could not be a true Christian and afraid of our family pet at the same time. Now, being a good Christian had paid off as my mom trusted me to go to the store by myself. This would be my first time being saved, in public!

Hey, Cutie

That day she let me go, I was focused on staying saved the entire two blocks. While I was singing saved songs, and thinking saved thoughts, a neighborhood boy drove up beside me on his bike.

"Hey, Cutie". I smiled because it was now my second experience being called cute in public. The first time was at my high school orientation a few weeks earlier. I was successful in maintaining my salvation there. All I had to do was keep my head in my Bible, ignore everyone and my salvation would be sure. I think my peers just thought I was weird. A boy told me I was cute, and I had no clue what to do other than read my Bible in hopes of a scripture verse to guide my path. I ignored the boy and all my peers that day, but when I left, I was like oh my goodness! Does being saved make me cuter? Am I allowed to be cute?

Now, I'm not going to lie, before I left the house, I asked Jesus if I could take a break from being saved to practice being cute. I felt like he said no. So when bike boy called me cute, I remained quiet and kept walking. "Oh yeah they said you're too cute to talk now. That's crazy. I knew you when you were ugly. I told them your stepdad is a racist cop and he probably beat you for being Black. That's why you stopped talking and you would have all those bruises all the time. But you can talk to me." That threw me off, so I responded. "No. I'm saved, and I don't talk to just anybody. I'm just trying to stay saved and go to the store." I kept walking.

He stopped in his tracks, and I was relieved until suddenly he was right behind me and knocked me down full force. I remember the rocky pavement feel. I remember I had made it on my walk as far as to the alley behind the candy store. I was almost there.

The God of My Salvation

"Okay, saved girl. You're still saved. You aren't doing anything wrong. I'm doing it to you, so talk to me! I bet you have something to say now..." that went on for minutes. I was still on the ground when he hopped on his bike and drove off. I was still on the ground, disheveled, trying to figure out if I was still saved or not.

Your walk with God is just that. A walk with Him. You can't act saved and do saved things.

Salvation is what happened to you. It's not a title. You get saved, you allow God to sanctify you or set you apart so you can become stable, firmly planted and secure in your walk with Christ.

You're Doing It Wrong

I had a few other traumatic incidents all happen around the time I gave my life to Christ. Those incidents never made me question or hate God. They did trip me up a bit. They made it clear I was doing something wrong. How did I get to such a wrong place in my walk with God when I started out so right?

There is a story in 1 Kings 13 about a very young man from Judah who became a prophet. He was brave. He was so brave; he went to deliver a dangerous message to the king. He was doing so well. On the way back, he decided to take a break. He had been given clear instructions on how to walk and what not to do... a small error – the break in his walk exposed him to what would eventually lead to his demise. He was walking along and got mauled by a lion. Not the ending I expected.

The thing about walking with God is that you have to walk with Him all the way. It's not a decision you can take lightly. It's not a decision you pick up at your convenience.

One thing I learned from the story in 1 Kings 13 and in real life is walking with God is a choice- it's the best choice you can make but is also a dangerous choice to make if you are not ready to fully commit. The young prophet did great until he did not. He decided eventually that his convenience was more important than the journey God was taking him on and as a result, his life was cut short. God is not for play play.

Sheri Asuoha

It's a Long Walk

I wanted to be saved and walk with God. More on my mind was a different journey. While there is nothing wrong with wanting to walk to the candy store, my mind was on being what my perception of a teenager was. Again that is not bad, but it is contrary to the decision I made. God had been speaking to me. He had given me things to write and do. Moments before I gave my life to Christ, He literally saved my life.

That day when biker boy attacked me in the back of the candy store, I'm sure his intention was to rape or violate me in some way. He was bigger than me. He was past the age of puberty and could have caused much damage.

I remember blocking him, but I was too stunned to fight. I remember him trying to tear my clothes. I remember the weight of his body on mine. I remember finally getting off the gravely ground after laying there for some time shocked, dirty, but unharmed. Of course I can't prove it, but I believe God was a shield for me. Wait, I got up unharmed. That is proof enough. God was and still is a shield for me.

YWM²

The beauty of walking with God is He does not stop walking with you. The danger of walking your own way after you made a choice to walk with Him is that you open yourself up to more threats than if you would have never began your walk in the first place. The devil is terrified of your decision. In fact, there is a way my pastor puts it- "There is nothing more dangerous to the devil than your decision".

I do not want to scare you away from following Christ. I just want to share with you that there is a strategy to it, so you don't make the same mistakes I did.

Walk WITH God

1. Walk with His guidance
2. Walk with everything He has equipped you with
   - *Grace*
   - *The Holy Spirit*
   - *Your assignment*
   - *Your instructions, prophecy*
   - *Your boundaries*
   - *Your testimonies*
   - *Access to the mercy and sovereignty of God*

Keep Walking

1. Don't stop
2. Don't detour
3. Don't be distracted

You might ask about taking a break. Your journey is designed by the Lord of the Sabbath Himself. Rest and pacing are your portion. Don't let the devil trick you into a mirage like he did the young prophet. He saw palm trees and esteem where there was really only distraction and deceit.

Just as there was a roaring lion waiting to attack the young prophet, there is one looking for the first opportunity to eat us who follow Christ alive. It says so in the Bible:

> *Be sober, be vigilant; because your adversary the devil walks about like a roaring lion, seeking whom he may devour.*
>
> **1 Peter 5:8**

Lessons From the Little Prophet Who Could... But Didn't

I started out like that young prophet, very strong, gifted, brave and anointed, rapping about Jesus to whoever would hear me. But I caved along the way. What is the difference between me and the young prophet? I am 36 at present to the glory of God. I had every opportunity to die in my youth.

YWM[2]

Good thing the Lion on our side is bigger, right? #LionOfJudah. But still, why did that young prophet die before his time while I still to declare the works of the Lord? I have done far worse things to get off track than take a break under a tree and trust a liar.

The young prophet deliberately disobeyed God after hearing His instructions clearly. He trusted himself and man more than God. He followed His flesh- which we have all been guilty of.

> [20]*While they were sitting at the table; the word of the LORD came to the old prophet who had brought him back.* [21] *He cried out to the man of God who had come from Judah, "This is what the LORD says:*
>
> *'You have defied the word of the LORD and have not kept the command the LORD your God gave you.* [22] *You came back and ate bread and drank water in the place where he told you not to eat or drink. Therefore your body will not be buried in the tomb of your ancestors.'"*
>
> **1 Kings 13:20-22**

But the issue was when God, in His mercy, brought His error to attention and warned him of the consequence. Look at what he does:

> [23]*When the man of God had finished eating and drinking, the prophet who had brought him back saddled his donkey for him.* [24] *...he went on his way*

Sheri Asuoha

1 Kings 13:23-24

…He went on his way. He got that word. He kept eating and drinking until he was finished, then got on his donkey like nothing happened and went along on his way. Keep walking, yes. But don't keep walking error. It's like missing your way and the GPS is telling you, please return to the route and you think if you just keep going, you will get there. You will get somewhere, but not the place you want to go.

> *24 As he went on his way, a lion met him on the road and killed him, and his body was left lying on the road, with both the donkey and the lion standing beside it. 25 Some people who passed by saw the body lying there, with the lion standing beside the body, and they went and reported it in the city where the old prophet lived. When the prophet who had brought him back from his journey heard of it, he said, "It is the man of God who defied the word of the LORD. The LORD has given him over to the lion, which has mauled him and killed him, as the word of the LORD had warned him." The prophet said to his sons, "Saddle the donkey for me," and they did so. 28 Then he went out and found the body lying on the road, with the donkey and the lion standing beside it. The lion had neither eaten the body nor mauled the donkey. 29 So the prophet picked up the body of the man of God, laid it on the donkey, and brought it back to his own city to mourn for him and bury him. 30 Then he laid the body in his own tomb, and they mourned over him and said, "Alas, my brother!" 31 After burying him, he said to his sons, "When I die, bury me in the grave where the man of God is buried; lay my bones beside his bones. 32 For the*

YWM²

message he declared by the word of the Lord against the altar in Bethel and against all the shrines on the high places in the towns of Samaria will certainly come true."

1 Kings 13:24-32

People wept for the young prophet. Miraculously, the lion did not eat him. The word he gave by the instruction of God would come to pass, but he did not get to enjoy any of it. What if as soon as he got that word from the old prophet, he repented and asked God for mercy?

One thing I learned in my dealings with God is that surely His goodness and mercy follows us. You just need to access it. I was the queen of giving up after I messed up. The devil wanted me to be accept failure and inadequacy. When God gives you the opportunity for correction, no matter how embarrassing or hopeless the situation looks, take it! Repent and do better with His help. You can come out of a sticky situation unscathed if you learn from your mistakes and choose not to give up on getting it right. If you need help on your walk, get help. Make sure it's God sent help. You are on a great journey. Walk accordingly.

Walk

She walked.
Through forests and hurts, Fears and pains.
She walked
Through storms of violence,
The cold of snow, sleet and rains
She walked
Though scorched,
Through piercing fires
She swam
Through toxic floods
Of feeling unwanted
She trekked the journey of the undesired.
It led her to what seemed a rugged and steep mountain of despair
Where winds whispered, "You won't make it," And she cried out in prayer.
"For so many years Lord I traveled this path.
The roads, filled with evils
The highways of wrath
I'm climbing, Lord
But You know I can't take it Much longer.
I'm trying so hard just to make it.
I need you to make me stronger
Please give me a sign so I know You are there."
Caringly the Lord answered,
I never put more on you than I know you can bear It is because I love you, I have lightened your load.
You will not stop until you finish.
You will make it
Keep walking this road.
Seasons passed

YWM²

As I walked
I walked many dark nights.
I was amidst the darkest hour
When my belly burst with light!
With that light came speed
With lightning speed
I ran 'til I reached the doorway! Before I entered my
prepared place, I took time to pray.
"As I walked through the valley of the shadows of death,
you breathed on me. I never lost breath.
I finished my course
With your help, my faith, I kept
You kept me when I whined
You were beside me as I wept.
Speaking spirit, your music that moved me. You gave me
strength with every inspirational talk, I thank you most
for guiding and walking beside me as I walked
And walked…And walked.

Sherilynn Asuoha

{6}

Learning to Fight

Fight the good fight for the true faith. Hold tightly to the eternal life to which God has called you, which you have declared so well before many witnesses.
1 Timothy 6:12

My grandmother would tell me stories. One of them was of her "Pitbull" days. When she was a child, everyone in her neighborhood called her "Pitbull" because of the violent, bulldog face she made as she took down the neighborhood bullies that tried to cross her.

Grandmother grew up in the projects of St. Louis, Missouri. The projects were full of stress, poverty and hard times.

But one day, my grandmother got the opportunity to go to Catholic school and the sisters there gave her special alter privileges. She took pleasure in having time away from the projects and she took great pride and had so much joy learning about God and serving Him as she took up assignments during mass services and helping the sisters. That place was her sanctuary, her safe space.

She was working for the Lord one afternoon when someone tried to pick a fight with her... in the sanctity of her school yard. She expected challenges in the projects, sure, but in her safe space? Hell no. Her boundary was officially crossed.

As she tells the story, it's as if God gave her supernatural strength that day. She put the church candles or whatever she was carrying down and put her fists up. She took down bully after bully until the sun went down. The kids kept coming to see if they could be the one to beat her. They were not.

Granny Fight!

Don't mess with our grandmothers because interestingly enough, my 75 year old mother-in-law had similar stories of fighting person after person in her youth and conquering them one by one. She did not want to fight, but, as she tells it, some people were hell bent on disturbing her peace. Meanwhile, the closest I ever got to a fight in my entire life was my Oreo situation. Why had I never been in a fight? Was there nothing in my life worth fighting for?

Worth Fighting For

Back in the day and even during much of my adult life, I decided I was not going to compete or work too hard for anything. I decided I had been through enough already. I used to work so hard on things and all it seemed to get me was stress, disappointment and scars. I had enough battle scars. So, I applied only to the schools I knew would accept me, not the school I desired. The first time around, I settled to marry a guy I did not love or feel safe with, but it was convenient and less stressful than waiting for a God-sent spouse I might never get. I did not think I was very pretty or wife material, so I did not believe I deserved much better than him anyway.

I was also very entitled. Despite the traumas I endured in early life, poverty and lack were not among them. My mother and stepfather worked hard to ensure we had any and everything we needed materially and more. While that was a good thing, it made it easy for me to learn to waste. Take what you want from me, I can always get something else, I rationed.

YWM²

Lazy Where?

This is the problem of many gifted people as well. Why fight or struggle to learn anything that is out of our comfort zone when so much comes naturally? I am creative and funny. I can write and act. But math intimidates me. Why learn it if I can find a major that allows me to avoid it at all costs? We don't see value in taking on what could end in failure. Such a mindset cost me relationships, valuable opportunities, lots of time and there were many skills I would need later that I did not bother to acquire because of the struggle it would take for me to master them.

A time came when God laid a very important assignment on my heart. I was excited to do it, but I did not have the stamina to compete with the challenges that came along with it. I asked God why I could not continue on though I really wanted to. He said, and I quote, "You are too lazy and careless to train and too weak to fight." I was most offended at the lazy part. I was a very hard worker. I worked full-time over nights, while walking to school every day as a high school student. I had 2-3 jobs in college while taking a full load plus extracurricular activity. Lazy where?

"You say I'm too lazy to fight? First of all," I thought to Him, "You kept me in situations where I was never in the position to fight. You left me to be a victim all those years and when I was finally big enough and wise enough to fight, aren't You the One who sheltered me? How come you never let me get in a fight at school or the playground? Even with my siblings- you made me like a mother to them. They fought each other, not me. Maybe I could be tougher if You gave me better life experiences."

Now that I am older and wiser in faith, I thank God He did not end my days sooner as I probably deserved. I was very ungrateful and very impatient with God at times. Yet He always took care of me, and He spoke to me. "I gave you several opportunities to train and you have been in many fights," He countered. "How many times did you give up before we began? How many times did you forget what we were training for…what we are fighting for?"

Epic Fails of a Preacher's Kid

My grandfather asked me to give the sermon in church for youth Sunday when I was about 15. I was both overwhelmed and over the moon. With everything in me,

YWM²

I wanted to be a teaching preacher. I was obsessed with scripture and apparently had said some things that made Grandfather think I was ready. I knew in my heart I was not. I was instantly overtaken with fear and reminders of why I shouldn't even be welcomed in church, talk less of speaking to them about Jesus while I was still trying to get it right with Him myself.

But still, I decided to ask God if I should accept the speaking assignment and what to do about it. He pointed me to Genesis 32:22-32:

> *²⁴ Then Jacob was left alone; and a Man wrestled with him until the breaking of day. ²⁵ Now when He saw that He did not prevail against him, He touched the socket of his hip; and the socket of Jacob's hip was out of joint as He wrestled with him. ²⁶ And He said, "Let Me go, for the day breaks." But he said, "I will not let You go unless You bless me!"*
>
> ***Genesis 32:22-32***

The fact that I got an answer from God was enough to take me from fear to flattery in moments. Did the Lord, Himself, just tell me what to preach? Watch out Ezekiel. There is a new prophet in town. I decided that God showing me this scripture was enough to confirm I should accept my grandfather's request.

Never mind what He wanted me to gain from the scripture. I had been around my grandfather and his pastor friends to serve, but maybe if I preached fire, I could sit amongst them- 15/16 years old, almost 5 ft. tall now, with braces- yes, I, too could be amongst the elders of the church and enjoy deep conversations about scripture and the state of the church today. I had 1000 ideas about how the church should be ran. Maybe this was my opportunity to qualify to speak.

Then I remembered I was terrified of public speaking. So I went from flattery back to fear again. I read the scripture over and over thinking of what to say. I was much too fearful and occupied to pray. On top of that, I was triggered. For a moment, I despised that particular scripture. Maybe because, Like Jacob, I had a bone broken by someone who was supposed to bless and protect me, too. I'm not sure. But instead of asking God what He wanted me to see in that passage, I decided to focus on my outfit for that Sunday to take my mind off things.

When I finally took time to pray, I knew what to say. I wrote it all down, but it was hardly anything. It was not profound or exciting. I had heard the messages my grandfather and His friends preached about blessings. This was not that

What God told me to say: (Pray, Read scripture) "When you feel alone, God is there, and He has a blessing for you. Jacob went through a lot and did some things wrong, but he never gave up until He got his blessing. He knew God was with him. Maybe if Jacob did not fight with Laban and wrestle with the angel, he wouldn't be blessing enough to bless us! His blessing came with a name change and a greater future than he could have ever imagined. It's a good thing he took it so seriously. Also, don't forget where your blessings came from. Sometimes, we get blessed and we forget, or we stop being grateful, but Jacob gave the place where he got his blessing a special name so that he wouldn't forget and so others would know about it and be blessed, too. So we should also have a special place where we meet and receive from God and thank Him for the blessings." (Pray. Call pastors for alter call. The end.)

Boring. I decided to spice it up a bit... let the men of God know that I was among them.

What 15 year old Sheri said instead: (Does not pray, instead remembers she has stage fright. Tries to overcompensate) Praise the Lord saints! I said praise the Lord saints! Praise God for Jacob's experience. But saints, I had a better experience. And you can have a better experience, too! One that does not require a hip replacement (crickets)! I got my blessing, but I didn't have to fight all night to get it. (Lists off a ton of accomplishments). When God spoke to me… yes, He, Himself visited me in a dream in the midnight hour (a lie- it was like 1:00 in the afternoon- and God said none of whatever I was talking about) and told me to preach to you from this scripture because I have gone through things in life, like Jacob did. So, I am qualified to preach to you today, but I didn't have to fight an angel or break my hip because I was already blessed. I am anointed. I am appointed for such a time as this! Just like Jacob, arrived at his blessing, I have arrived. This is my blessing. Praise the Lord." (drops mic and runs to the back of the church)

While I was hiding, I expected to at least hear crickets, but no. Even they were speechless. Thank God my grandfather was wise enough not to let me speak on the actual alter. A pastor came behind me to clean it all up. And my grandfather apologized to the church on my behalf. They made a joke about it.

Don't Fight for the Victory. Fight to Defend It.

Days later, after I sobered up from that whole experience, God took me on a journey through the book of Joshua where I learned that the Israelites still had to fight for the land God gave them. They had the victory, but they had to stay in the will of God, and they had to fight. Oh. That's where I went wrong in my first sermon, among other things. That speaking opportunity was actually an opportunity to overcome many things including stage fright. But rather than go through the process- a process that included being the first partaker of the word the Holy Spirit was bringing my attention to, I avoided it, distracted myself with what did not matter, etc.

God was trying to change my mindset about fighting and what to fight for. I would have known that if I was not so distracted by the opportunity for platform. I was about to face many battles and I eventually lost many of them because I didn't see enough value in what I was fighting for to train properly or even enter the ring.

The Teeny, Teeny Woman

There is another story my grandmother used to tell me that I would like to share with you. It's called, "The Teeny, Teeny Woman". If you have ever heard or used the term, "I have a bone to pick with you," when you are about ready to fight someone, this story gives great context to it.

Sheri Asuoha

Once upon a time, there was a teeny, teeny, woman. And the teeny, teeny woman lived in a teeny, teeny house. The teeny, teeny house was on a teeny, teeny street where there also lived a great, big, dog. In, the great, big dog's house, was a great big bone that the great big dog placed in a great big pot to make some stew. "Teeny, teeny woman, I am going out. Whatever you do, don't touch my bone. I know you want it, but I got it first. You can't have it. if you touch it, there's gonna be a fight." And the great big dog went on his way. The teeny, teeny woman was very hungry. "I have no food," she said to herself, "I wish I got that bone first." She looked out the window and into the Great, Big Dog's house to see the great, big pot in the great, big dog's window. In the pot, the bone was shining. "That's it. I am going to get that bone and make something to eat." So she quickly ran over, took the bone and ran home to eat. The teeny, teeny woman ate and ate until she was full and suddenly, she heard a voice. It was the Great, big dog. "Teeny, teeny woman, I know you took my bone. I am coming for you! Teeny, Teeny woman, I'm on the first step." The Teeny, teeny woman panics and hides behind her door. "Teeny, teeny woman, I'm on the second step." The teeny woman becomes very, very afraid and hides under her bed. "Teeny, teeny woman, I'm at your doorstep". By now the teeny woman is terrified. "Teeny, teeny, woman, I got you!"

The story would end in tickling and play- but while I was laughing and giggling, even as a little girl, I was always left wondering. Did this little woman really go through all that because of a bone? Why was the dog commanding the woman and not the other way around? My biggest question was what was the true moral of the story? Was it a lesson not to steal? I always thought it had to do with either not stealing or learning to find better hiding spaces if you do plan to steal. But really, it was a lesson on limits.

The Teeny, Teeny Woman, was not just small in stature. She was small in mindset. Afterall, small as she was, she was still a human being, yet she was contending with a dog to get what she needed.

Even The Dogs

When I think of the teeny woman in this story, I can't help but compare her to the crying woman in Matthew 15 who was also in desperate need. By the time she came to Jesus she had been through hell, literally. She was the mother and sole caretaker of a child possessed by a demon. I am going to highlight a few key parts of this story but read it all for context.

> *21 Then Jesus went out from there and departed to the region of Tyre and Sidon. 22 And behold, a woman of Canaan came from that region and cried out to Him,*

saying, "Have mercy on me, O Lord, Son of David! My daughter is severely demon possessed." But He answered her not a word. And His disciples came and urged Him, saying, "Send her away, for she cries out after us." But He answered and said, "I was not sent except to the lost sheep of the house of Israel." Then she came and worshiped Him, saying, "Lord, help me!" But He answered and said, "It is not good to take the children's bread and throw it to the little dogs." And she said, "Yes, Lord, yet even the little dogs eat the crumbs which fall from their masters' table." Then Jesus answered and said to her, "O woman, great is your faith! Let it be to you as you desire." And her daughter was healed from that very hour.

Matthew 15:21- 24

Before she got what she needed, she had to travel out of her comfort zone. A football team full of men blocked her from seeing Jesus and made it clear she was not welcome and important. Even after all that, she persisted. She begged for mercy only for the man she came to see to tell her she was not worth the miracle she so desperately needed- or at least that's what the devil wanted her to hear.

I want to pause for a moment so we can digest the magnitude of what it is like to be in distress and feel rejected, ignored and worthless. I felt like this most of my childhood and even much of my adult life. It seemed the people I most expected to be in my corner found reason to dismiss me. Grant it, I may have given them reason, but still, it is painful. She went through all that, but she had enough audacity to get what she came for.

There are three reasons that lady was able to get what she needed. One reason is found in Matthew 15:21b. *"Even the dogs eat..."* That tells me she knows she is better than a dog and has no reason to be bothered with being compared to one. In fact, she basically said, "Look here, Jesus, you want to compare me to a dog? Fine. Even the dogs are worthy of crumbs from the master's table. If a dog is worthy crumbs... even as a Gentile, I am worthy of much more..."

Another reason she succeeded is because she had an agenda to keep her focused. When your mind is on what you need to accomplish, you don't have time to worry about offense or obstacles. All your energy is on taking the necessary steps to get what you set out to get. But the first and most important reason she succeeded is found in the often overlooked portion of Matthew 15:21. It is the most important step she took, and it is this step that has been the game changer for my personal life. I am going to give us verse 20b and 21a for context:

> *He (Jesus) replied, "It is not right to take the children's bread and toss it to the dogs." And she said, "Yes, Lord..."*

Cultivate a habit of agreeing with Jesus and it changes how you experience things. When Jesus said what He said, she basically said amen and that gave her the platform to declare what would lead to her victory. If the Word of the Lord remains your foundation and motivation, you become an unstoppable force.

God forbid any of us ever have to fight a dog for a bone. But if it has to do with your blessing or your destiny, fight like your life depends on it because it does. Fight with the word of God and remember you are not fighting alone.

{7}

Stewardship

For even the Son of Man did not come to be served, but to serve, and to give His life a ransom for many."
Mark 10:45

*But, why though? -**Sheri***

Let me ask those of you who know you are on a great journey a question. What's the most important part of your walk with Christ (Besides Jesus)? A hint towards my personal answer and a great pre-cursor to this chapter is found in Mark 4:8 and Matthew 25:14-30. Read those before moving on.

Earlier in this book, I told you I used to lose many things as a child. When I got older, not much changed. One thing I used to lose a lot was my keys. In my early twenties, after leaving a HORRIBLE relationship and an awkward roommate situation, I finally got my own place. It wasn't much, just a small studio, but I liked it because it was by the lake and very close to public transportation, the liquor store, and good Chinese food.

Keys Open Doors

While enjoying my newfound freedom, I developed this habit of leaving my keys in the keyhole of my apartment unit door every night. My unit was small, but the apartment complex, itself was quite large with many others living inside. I lived in Chicago. If you know anything about Chicago, you can understand how problematic it might be to leave your keys outside your door.

When I would come home on a good day, it was very late. But most days, I returned in the middle of the night or when night was just reaching dawn. I was either tired from work, drunk out of my mind, or deep in thought. Maybe my hands were full of groceries, who knows. I had 101 excuses as to why I'd forget my keys. Eventually, I got used to hearing knocks on my door in the twilight hours.

"Ma'am. your keys...".

"Oh, my bad," I'd apologize. And the whole situation would repeat two days later.

YWM²

One night I was on my futon, dozing off after some homework and vodka when something said, *check your door.* But I was comfortably on my futon. Grant it, it was literally only one step from my futon to my studio door, but what if someone was there? What if I got up and could not be as comfortable as I felt in that moment. It was easier to sleep while I was in the position and mood to do so, lest I get up and actually have to do some adulting.

The next morning I awoke, took my morning Tequila shot, and was getting ready for my day. I had work, internship and class. So, it's likely I took two Tequila shots. I couldn't find my keys. I looked everywhere. I searched high and low... all of which took two minutes because that's how big my studio was. Then I remembered, *Oh. They are probably in the door.*

I opened the door prepared to grab my keys. They were not there. Instead, there was an unsigned sticky note filled with explicative language in the most hostile handwriting I'd ever seen. It was from one of my neighbors about my bad habit. I wondered which neighbor had the audacity. I was already running behind schedule. I would run even more behind because I needed another Tequila shot to mentally prepare for the added stress.

"#@$%#$! Y'all just gone take my keys?! Whatever." I knocked on doors to see if anyone had seen my keys. Of course, no one admitted to taking them. Great. Now, I had to go talk to the property manager, which would require yet another shot of Tequila. The property manager was a really, really old lady from an unknown European country far, far away. She lived in a studio not much bigger than my own in the same complex, but she acted like she owned the place. She talked too much. She did way too much. I felt she just needed to sit down, collect the rent and help us get into our apartments when we were locked out instead of stressing over things people were just going to mess up again anyway.

"Good afternoon, ma'am. Sorry to bother you. I know you are really busy," I greeted.

"Do you see this? I keep telling people, 'Don't force this gate before the elevator door opens. Now, look. It's stuck and we have to fix it because everybody is in a rush. Carelessness!"

"Right, these people are so careless. It's such a shame. Well, I don't want to keep you from all this that you're dealing with, but someone in this building took my keys.

YWM²

It's just like you said, people are so careless! Anyway, I could just keep leaving my door unlocked, you know, so I don't have to keep bugging you to let me in. But it's really an inconvenience and unsafe if I have to keep doing that. Since it's my first time asking, can I get another key for free, or do you happen to have an extra copy I can borrow for a while? If not, how much is it going to cost? I really can't afford anything too crazy right now."

There I was trying to be relatable and appeal to her humanity as a victim of circumstances. What did I get in return? Her eyes. The way she looked through me hurt. Her her green, judgmental, old lady eyes slashed my entitlement in half and pierced my soul and my Tequila was nowhere within reach.

"You say you can't afford anything... but you can afford to be drunk every time, right?"

Now hold on just a minute...

"You can afford to leave your keys where somebody can take them. Young lady... you are just renting, worried about something that doesn't even cost you anything. Worried about your inconvenience, but you don't care how much it will cost the person who owns this place to reset the locks to keep all the tenants safe. You don't care what it costs your neighbors if somebody breaks in our building with your keys. Some of them have children! Do you know what it's costing me to stop what I'm doing because of you..." she kept talking.

I really was trying to listen respectfully; she was making some valid points. But then I remembered... OMG... my car keys. The keys to my beloved were on that key ring.

When I broke up with my ex, besides my laptop and all 100 of my books, the one thing I bargained to keep were the keys to my beloved, glittery, black Jeep Grand Cherokee. We'd named her Black Cherry. I was still paying an over-priced, high interest rate car note on my beloved.

Every other week or so, Chicagoans are required to move our cars to the opposite side of the street for street cleaning. I didn't have my keys. I couldn't move my truck. The property manager was still lecturing me.

They eventually towed my truck, and I didn't have the funds to get her out of impound. I was crushed and subjected to public transportation. As much as I was not

YWM²

(and still am not) a fan of publicly shared anything, I spent a lot of time downtown for work and school and there was never parking anyway. Traffic was always horrible. I shrugged my shoulders… and never even went to say goodbye to my beloved. *Goodbye, Black Cherry.* I said in my heart. *Don't expect me to keep paying that car note, though.*

For the remainder of my time in that studio apartment, I gave up my right to enter at will. I came and went at the mercy of those more responsible. My ex ended up getting Black Cherry out of impound and keeping her. I think he renamed her, Onyx. I didn't sweat it. I sucked it up and moved on with my life because, I thought, at the end of the day, the truck, as much as I loved her, was never really mine. The apartment lease was in my name, but I did not own a square inch of that place. I was a supervisor in my place of employment, true, but it was not my business. They were upgrading to an electronic locking system anyway. Losing those keys didn't cost me a thing. Like the old property manager lady said… and is probably still saying- all of it costed the true owners much more.

Sheri Asuoha

John The Janitor

Let me tell you this story I heard about a janitor. One year, I was required to attend a regional stewardship conference as a leader- in- training at my former church. That was right after the first year I made a decision to give God everything. I had just received the coveted *Rookie of the Year Stewardship Award*. Very Prestigious. But I wanted to find out just how much more stewardly I could become so I was happy to be at this conference.

This man of God takes a session at the conference and tells us the story about a janitor. Oh, but he was no ordinary janitor.

The pastor of this janitor's church received a sudden word from the Lord to host a special healing meeting one Sunday evening after everyone had already left church and gone home. He immediately informed his leaders about the word he received from God and gave each leader instructions to carryout in preparation for the special service, acknowledging that he understood they did not have much time.

His ordained leaders were very caught off guard. Some of them were heading to work for their shifts.

YWM²

Others already had plans. Those who did not have plans had transportation issues, etc. The pastor understands with his leaders. He was only surprised that not one of them was available and saw it, not as coincidence, but as a matter to pray about.

But he could not pray that prayer in that moment. He needed to carry out all the tasks he had given to his associate ministers to ensure things were ready for the meeting that was now just a few hours away. He invited the members. Contacted the praise and worship leaders. He gave them the songs God had placed on his heart.

What next? He needed to make sure the atmosphere was set in the meeting space. He heads to the meeting room speaking in tongues. He flicks on the lights. The lights don't come on. As if things can't get any worse, he hears buzzing sounds. Something is fluttering around. There is a window letting in some light as the sun goes down. On that window are a number of wasps or hornets indicating there is likely a nest somewhere in the area where the meeting must take place.

The Pastor takes a deep breath, walks out of the meeting space and continues to walk around the building, praying, asking God to give him direction concerning the meeting. His associate pastors continue to text him their excuses and prayer requests as he is praying. A few minutes into his tongues, he drops to his knees in worship and God tells him to get up and go quickly back to that meeting room. *The room with the hornets? Yes, Lord.* He doesn't hesitate- and it's a good thing, too. As soon as he gets there, he sees a figure in the darkness. By now the sun has set. He hears the buzzing of the wasps and something that sounds like heavenly tongues.

The figure was strong and tall, and seemed very fierce, like an angel ascending in the middle of the room. God had told him something special was going to happen this night... He expected an encounter... but this? The pastor was almost speechless, but he had to be sure of what he was seeing. He dropped to his knees and cried out, "Lord, is this really You? Your servant is here!"

Ah, who am I Lord that You will visit me like this? What a wonderful thing! I so wish my ministers were here! He said in his heart.

The heavenly tongues that buzzed from the divine shadow before him halted, almost abruptly intensifying the violent buzzing of the wasps. "Ah, Pastor, It's me, John, your janitor, Sir. Please Sir, pray with me! There's a hornets nest up here, Sir! I didn't know before I climbed up!!"

YWM²

"For heaven's sake, get down!" The pastor shouted as he rushed to his feet.

"Sir, I was told you have an urgent meeting tonight! I came to check on the meeting space and found that the light bulb needed to be changed."

"Okay, come down!"

"I'm not done changing the light bulb, Sir"

"Chineke..." the pastor thinks aloud, placing his hands on his head in disbelief. Yes, it was much easier believing it was the Angel of the Lord, there meeting him in the darkness, than it was to believe how serious this man was about changing a light bulb.

"My pastor, please pray so I can change it, before these hornets consume me, please," The pastor was appalled but he began to pray in tongues until John, the Janitor fixed the light.

The janitor is getting all kinds of stung. "Please, flip the lights, Sir," the pastor ran to flip the light switch and behold, there was light. "Praise God! Thank you, Heavenly Father," John worshipped. "Thank you, Jesus! Now come down, please!"

John the Anointed Janitor climbed down, covered in hornet stings, he nearly passes out. The pastor prays for his healing. He recovers immediately and goes home (or I think that's how it ended- I don't know. I never got past which kind of janitorial anointing carries flying insects and light bulbs on a ladder, in the dark while speaking in tongues).

Stewarding to Death

I was still digesting that story when the man of God started with another. This one was from the Bible. I guess he felt like he really needed to hammer it into our hearts how serious we needed to take our stewardship. He ministered to us from 1 Samuel 31:4. At this point, King Saul had accepted defeat. In this account of his death, Saul refused to die at the hands of the Philistines. He tells his armor bearer to thrust his sword into his chest and kill him. The armor bearer is like, "Umm... no,". So, Saul does it himself. When the armorbearer realizes King Saul was dead serious (pun intended) he followed suit.

I didn't expect all these stories of faithful stewards to end with stewards so loyally committed, they stewarded themselves to death. But, like a good steward, I took it all in. I took notes. I had a couple of thoughts concerning all I heard, though. And I wrote them down along with the prayer points I felt should accompany them.

YWM²

Thought 1: Wow, these stewards were very committed... I definitely need to be more committed.

Prayer Point: God, give me a loyal and committed heart that I might be a better steward, in Jesus' name. Amen.

Thought 2: Yes, I am ready to be more committed. I want to be so committed that I am ready to die to get the job done. (Pause) But, as I think about it, God delivered me from the spirit of suicide not too long ago. I can't go back to where you brought me from. If I die, who's going to change the proverbial light bulb?

Prayer Point: Lord, I shall not die, but live to declare the works of the Lord, in Jesus' name. Amen.

Thought 3: Come to think of it, the anointing wasn't even on Saul when he decided to die and let all his loyal stewards die with him. He died without a legacy and in response to a curse. His armor bearer wasn't noble, he was stupid just like his dead, no- anointing- having leader.

Prayer Point: I will not die a stupid death trying to advance another man's dead, no- anointing- no- oil having program, IJN.

There. Those prayers should help me be the kind of steward God is looking for. The Lord smiled and pointed me to this scripture:

> *"Have this attitude in yourselves which was also in Christ Jesus, who, although He existed in the form of God, did not regard equality with God a thing to be grasped, but emptied Himself, taking the form of a bond-servant, and being made in the likeness of men.*
>
> ***Philippians 2:5-8***

But when I read it the first time, I couldn't help but think about this scripture:

> *"Thomas, nicknamed the Twin, said to his fellow disciples, "Let's go, too—and die with Jesus."*
>
> ***John 11:16***

As a recovering professor of sarcasm, I know that behind every sarcastic joke is a hint of truth. I totally felt Thomas's truth in that moment when he was compelled to do the right thing by the mercy of God though his heart was filled with fear and doubt. As reasonable as Thomas' remark was (given that particular circumstance), it's never the right mindset for effective stewardship, followership or leadership.

YWM²

It's a privilege to serve the Lord and it leads to a great reward. We have to understand that or else we are only serving in vain. God is the one we are serving. He is a rewarder. It pleases Him when we know that about Him and act accordingly.

I have a confession. I was one of the people who needed to do all the things and be in all the departments. I used to lie to myself. I lied to myself for so long, I began to believe the lie: *As long as I overwork myself until everybody sees it, then I am in the will of God.* I was "stewarding" myself to death like the stupid armor bearer, serving and committing to causes in ignorance or that had nothing to do with me and my destiny. That lead to burn out. It lead to me feeling empty, unappreciated and even stupid on the inside. But I kept going, because it was the right thing to do, right? It made me loyal and committed as a steward should be.

Or maybe, it made me appear to be more sanctified than my actual intimate time with Christ was. Maybe I felt deep down, serving in the sanctity of my local church was safer and less degrading than serving God as He truly required of me. If people can't see how I am serving, what will that do to my reputation and how will I have earned the coveted rookie steward of the year award?

Sheri Asuoha

Slave Vs. Steward

While I was being steward of the year, I was dismissed from my doctoral program. I was so overwhelmed, I resigned from my role as the youngest director my organization ever had. My job was actually where God needed me to minister the most at that time. Hence, he placed me in a leadership position I wasn't even qualified for. I neglected my position at work, I neglected research I'd just received IRB approval for in school leading to my dismissal, I neglected some less visible stewardship responsibilities I had editing a Christian blog.

I buried them just like that guy I told you to read about at the beginning of this chapter (Matthew 25:14-30). He buried what was entrusted to his care the second he looked around and saw he only had 1 talent while his fellow servants had more. He buried what was entrusted to his care the second he realized what he had was not only small, but it also wasn't even his! It's hard enough to only have a little bit to work with. Why should I toil and stress over what is only going to advance another man's program? That is the kind of question you ask when you have no program. It's the best kind of question you can ask if you've decided to remain a slave.

YWM²

Look at the words below. They are not the same.

FIGURE 1: STEWARDSHIP PROGRESSION

We all start out as slaves to one thing or the other. But you should be ready to move from that stage as swiftly as possible. Being a slave is easy. You get to blame everything on whatever or whoever you are enslaved to. As a slave, you can rest assured you'll always get enough to survive and do the bare minimum required of you. Being a slave is also a waste of your God given time and value. There is no reward for you in slavery. Anything that does not yield reward for you, God is not in it.

It is good to be a servant. It's a critical and life-long phase we all must engage on our great journey. When you serve, you gain the mind of Christ. You learn how to please God. You learn how to treat people and care for things. Jesus tells us the significance of this phase in the scripture I will share with you in the next section of this chapter.

But, beloved, there is a whole world God needs to trust us to care about and care for. Stewardship means you have mastered the art of caring and loving and valuing at the God-level. When you become a steward, you become a producer. You become the kind of leader that can reproduce, enhance and further your master's vision. You become what God created you to be as described in Genesis 1:26-28.

Stewardship: Reputation Vs. Destination

Before I knew better, I engaged stewardship as if it were my reputation: it was the way I needed people to see me. It was what I wanted people to know me for. The proper way to engage stewardship is as a destination; it has everything to do with where you are going in this life and the one beyond. If you understand that you were created to reign… if you understand you were created in the likeness and image of GOD… and that you were not put here to survive and make it to heaven, then what I am saying about how we must engage stewardship as a destination should make sense. If it does not, I trust God to give you this revelation- and quickly- in Jesus' mighty name.

YWM²

Remember the scripture I told you God said I should look at after the stewardship conference I attended- the one found in Philippians 2:5-8? Let me give you a heads up about it. When you engage that scripture, the most detrimental thing you can do as a child of God is stop at verse 8. If you are content to stop there, you've missed the whole message. Let's look at the instruction again and in its full context:

> *Let this mind be in you, which was also in Christ Jesus, who, being in the form of God, did not consider it robbery to be equal with God, but made Himself of **no reputation**, taking the form of a bondservant, and coming in the likeness of men. And being found in appearance as a man, He humbled Himself and became obedient to the point of death, even the death of the cross. **Therefore, God also has highly exalted Him and given Him the name, which is above every name,** that at the name of Jesus every knee should bow, of those in heaven, and of those on earth, and of those under the earth, and that every tongue should confess that Jesus Christ is Lord, to the glory of God the Father.*
>
> *Philippians 2:5-8*

Saints, it's the ***therefore*** for me. I included verses 10-11 just because I love reminding Satan of those, but I really just want you to get two things from this passage. Do you see how Jesus made Himself of no reputation? He was on a great journey. He decided His mission was bigger than making a name for Himself. He knows His Father as a rewarder and as the One who gives everything name and purpose. Jesus knows His Father and Master as the only One whose opinion matters in the grand scheme of things. When you know your Master always has your future and best interest in mind... when you know it's His nature and passion to reward you, every sacrifice you make as His Servant and the steward of all He has entrusted to you is a privilege.

We see the same energy in Hebrews 11. In that letter to the Hebrews, the writer spits 40 solid bars about people whose lives sound like tragedies until you understand that they were not playing the same natural game of life everyone else was playing. I like how the New Living Translation puts it:

> *...destitute and oppressed and mistreated. **38** They were too good for this world, wandering over deserts and mountains, hiding in caves and holes in the ground. **39** All these people earned a good reputation because of their faith, yet none of them received all that God had promised. **40** For God had something better in mind for us, so that they would not reach perfection without us.*
>
> **Hebrews 11:37b-40**

Their mindsets were eternal. They were thinking like God. In other words, they reached a point in life where they chose to allow their thinking to transcend what was basic and natural. They took on that mind of Christ we read about in Philippians (Yes, those Old Testament Hall of Faith Inductees enjoyed the mind of Christ before Christ manifested physically as savior of the world) and they decided that everything they did and desired would move God's program in heaven and on earth. Their stewardship transcended serving in leading all the ministry departments in church. Praise God for those critical assignments- but if that's where it stops, you need to level up.

And did you see that word *reputation* again in Hebrews 11:39? Those Hall of Faith inductees were going somewhere. Stewardship was their mindset- a kingdom value that helped them get to where they were going in God's program for their life.

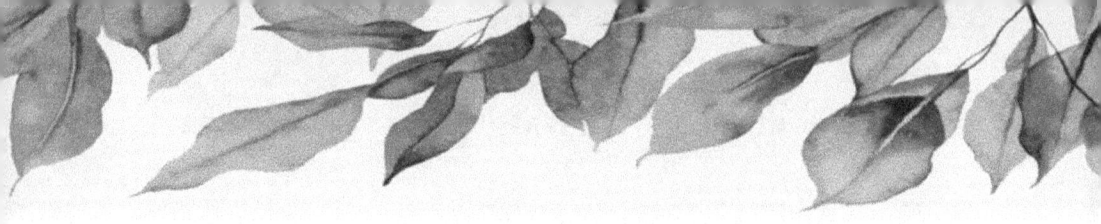

{8}
Stewardship II: YWM²

Because you are sons, God has sent the Spirit of His Son into our hearts, crying out, "Abba! Father!" 7 Therefore you are no longer a slave, but a son; and if a son, then an heir through God.
Galatians 4:6-7

I was ordained to the office of the deaconate in 2014. Five years later I resigned. Well, I tried to resign. I thought it was the right thing to do because I did not feel qualified. My pastorate listened caringly as I gave them my rationale for quitting. They validated my feelings and ministered to me. They wanted me to be certain I understood the implications of what I was doing. They also wanted me to know how the devil operates. Satan will do and help you believe anything to keep you from the will of God for your life.

My pastors and other leaders in the church prayed with me and encouraged me to rest in God's presence before I made my final decision. As I rested and prayed, I received answers of peace from God. He gave me blessed assurance and warned me that there was safety in my appointment. God basically warned me that I needed to stay as close to the alter as possible. I needed all the grace and anointing I could get! My life and destiny depended on it. The rest of the leaders rejoiced and encouraged me to stay planted and to trust God's plans for my life more than I trusted my own doubts and fears. They told me I was valuable and many other positive, uplifting things that I obviously did not internalize because two years later, I resigned again.

River

I wrote my resignation as eloquently as I possibly could.

Dear Pastorate,

Thank you for all you have instilled in me... I don't take the calling for granted. However, I think it is in my best interest to hang up. I appreciate the oil you poured on my head and the anointing and impartation and all of that, but I no longer desire to use them for the office you assigned me to and therefore I resign. Oh, I will still be a steward- meaning I will do my preferred activities in church to fulfill all righteousness. I am still a 'son' in the house, so I will still call you for what I need you for. But I will no longer operate under that leadership assignment you gave me because there are far too many risks involved with it. I am too flawed. I am stressed and I have too much at stake. Why would you trust me to be on your leadership team anyway? Before you fire me, before all my weaknesses are exposed and before I risk losing everything that is important to me, including my mind, I quit. Thank you for understanding.

I resigned because I was having those same feelings Thomas had- feelings of fear... doubt... uncertainty. I was four months pregnant and over 35 years old. I wore many hats but only one of those hats mattered to me at the time. Church (any) people, no matter how much you love them can drive you crazy if you let them, especially if you lead them with your flesh... or with your fears. The moment I pushed the "return" button launching my resignation letter into cyberspace or however emails travel, I felt odd. I went to the restroom to check myself out. Something was not right. Sure enough, I was bleeding. I texted my sister, the dreamer of the family and a registered nurse. She told me it was normal. But I knew what I was feeling was not normal. I texted my pastors. I don't even know why. Maybe because one of them was a Nurse Practitioner. Maybe I hoped they would tell me something better than I already knew. They tried to. Or maybe they truly believed all would be well. Maybe they were annoyed at my resignation. Maybe I no longer qualified for whatever grace might spare me from the inevitable.

Two days later, I gave birth to a baby who was clearly far too good for this world in a dated hospital bathroom[18]. Shortly after giving birth to a baby I could never see or hold, I received a letter from my pastor accepting my letter of resignation.

The Cost of Stewardship

John the Baptist, Thomas and many stewards of God chosen for these great ministry experiences must feel some type of way about having to minister and serve God in the area of their weakness and deficiency. I know I did. That's why I quit. Jesus charged Thomas to go around preaching the gospel knowing he struggled with doubt. John The Baptist was supposed to go around telling people that the One with the authority to set captives free had arrived meanwhile he was sitting in jail. I'm anointed to teach, heal and minister through writing. I'm still learning, hurting, and writing has yet to

---

[18] I named her ***River*** in accordance with John 7:38 just to make sure the Devil knew he was a liar.

be as profitable to me as I or my very Igbo husband would appreciate.

When we minister as God tells us to, how He tells us to, despite our feelings or the lack of convenience of it all, that's the sacrifice of stewardship. He knew our weaknesses before He called us. We and are submitted frailties are the perfect vessel for Him to manifest His strength. Don't think you're not qualified or get angry and give up because of your weaknesses or your vulnerabilities. Don't try to overcompensate for them either. Surrender them to God with the rest of the life you said you gave Him.

It's Not For Them To Know

Shortly, after I received my pastors email accepting my resignation, I tried to be okay with it until I wasn't. *What happened to all the compassion and nurture he showed me the last time? Oh well, maybe is for the best,* I thought. At the violent and I guess merciful unction of the Holy Spirit, I recanted my resignation. Sidebar- this is why it is so important to feed your Spirit. You need it to be louder than your flesh. If I told you how my flesh preferred to respond, you would look at me different. The Holy Spirit in me allowed me to submit when logically and emotionally I was entitled to stay home, grieve and thank God for the burden lifted with all the other time commitments I had.

By now, my pastor had already announced to the rest of the leadership team that he was accepting my resignation. My flesh said, "To be honest, this is best for everyone." My Spirit said, "Follow my instructions". Sure enough that night, my First lady gave me some instructions. I laughed. But I feared the Holy Spirit enough to comply. It lead to a meeting where I wanted simply to apologize and move forward. But at a point, my flesh rose up.

"I was in a hospital bed ministering to people. I was very sick, and I was afraid. No one called to pray for me, (*no one was sensitive enough to pray I wouldn't lose my child or maybe no one cared or even cared to know what I was going through*) but I called how many people to pray with them, give them prophecies, celebrate testimonies of prophesies fulfilled with them. I checked on them. No one talks about that. We just get mad because I expressed myself. We care more about protocols than actual people. You have no idea what I go through or what I sacrifice. Respectfully, calling is irrevocable so cancel me or re- install me or kick me out of the church I am here in obedience to the Holy Spirit to state my initial action was inconsiderate. Title or not I'm the same Sheri who does more than you know and not because of this leadership role. I am a leader by standard".

My pastors looked at me and smiled almost as if to say, "Okay. Join the club." It's not for people to know and see everything you do and all you are going through as you do serve and do what God requires of you as His servant. How ratchet would it be if you went to a restaurant, ordered a meal and was required to hear and validate the account of all it to for your server to serve you that day. I think it would make it harder to enjoy the meal, defeating the very purpose of the server's existence. But we do that with our pastors and people in our departments all the time. We need to know that they know everything it took for us to minister. I put the word 'minister' there instead of 'serve' or 'make it to choir rehearsal on time', so it would hit different.

People won't know the battle's you are fighting while you are ministering and striving to please God and be an example and way of escape. Your journey is peculiar to you, beloved. You will kill yourself and waste your time trying to make people to understand the peculiarity of your walk with Christ.

So Anxious

After I had my revelation about stewardship, I began to see the areas where I served the Lord and carried out assignments as a sanctuary and not a threat. I guess the devil figured that out. So he started to disturb me very specifically in those areas by blurring the lines between what God assigned me to do and what I decided I should be doing in the place of assignment. Once that happened, it became easy for Satan to make it look like doing the work of God was dangerous and a threat to things I held as very important. I became quite anxious and almost paranoid even as a minister.

John the Baptist became so anxious at a point, too, and rightfully so! Things were not making sense and his life was literally on the line. Rather than asking the very Jesus he preached about- the very Jesus he said was so great he wasn't worthy to tie his shoes or however the verse goes-, he did the same thing I fell into the trap of doing 2000 years later. He did it to his little cousin, Jesus. I did it to the person I chose and vowed to serve under: this thing where we passive aggressively deflect our fear onto everyone else as condescendingly as we possibly can in hopes of getting the help or support we think we need, how we need it, without making ourselves look weak:

> **2 When John, who was in prison, heard about the deeds of the Messiah, he sent his disciples 3 to ask him, "Are you the one who is to come, or should *we* expect someone else?"**
>
> ***Matthew 11:2-3***

Who is the "we" he was talking about when it was only him with fears and insecurities and in need of help. He knew Jesus was doing wonders. He knew others were having life changing experiences and enjoying the deeds of the Messiah as evident by the reports, he just heard.

Before, he zealously served and acknowledged Jesus as his Lord and Savior. Now, he was asking the same person if He was who He said he was.

What I am about to say is very important. There are four things that- above all, you must be a good steward of: Your time, your resources, your words and your relationship. Allow me to say it in another way. There are four things you must value as if your life depends on it: your time, your resources, your words and your relationships. I think the first two are self-explanatory. But these last two are where we find ourselves in trouble and they're probably why John got his head cut off.

Word Power

We have what we say. You might know that. But understand we have what we say, how we say it, too. When you look deeply into the letter John wrote to Jesus, and having all the context, you will understand that John was likely writing from a place of fear and frustration, and he wanted Jesus's help. Maybe we translate it like this:

Dear Jesus,

I am in prison, about to die. How is your day going? I guess you know I'm in jail. I'm sure God told you was going on with me. I just wondered because I am still sitting in prison, still telling everyone about you from prison, meanwhile, you, my cousin, and savior of the world are doing good deeds and helping everyone but me. But it's cool, though. I am so glad to hear about all the great things you are doing, and that people are finding out who you really are. I just think it's funny that I am the one who risked my life in the wilderness to prepare the way for all this to happen. I am the one who told people the truth in your name. Now, I am the one sitting in prison, about to die for trying to help you set captives free and gain eternal life. The irony. Anyway, I just thought you should know how I feel because right now I'm afraid and could use some assurance. Please give me an answer of peace.

Love,

Big Cousin, John the Baptist

    Of course, the above is what he meant- it's even the truth. But when he wrote what he wrote, how he wrote it according to Matthew 11:2-3- this is what he said, invariably:

Dear Little Cousin Whom I Paved the Way For,

I feel like I wasted my life serving you because based on my situation right now, it's obvious You aren't all You claim to be and if You are, You aren't acting like it. I started ministering years before you. Don't forget, people know me. They are just getting to know You, which means there is plenty of room for doubt and I can cause it just by virtue of this letter I am sending through my disciples. Beware of my influence and prove me wrong by attending to my cause.

John THEE Baptist.

YWM²

...And resultantly, John got a response commensurate with the tone and texture of the words he had his disciples deliver to Jesus:

> *Jesus replied, "Go back and report to John what you hear and see: The blind receive sight, the lame walk, those who have leprosy] are cleansed, the deaf hear, the dead are raised, and the good news is proclaimed to the poor. Blessed is anyone who does not stumble on account of me."*
>
> ***Matthew 11:4-6***

Period. And as far as scripture tells us, this is the end of their earthly relationship with one another. This is where the value of relationship comes into play. John addressed Jesus like his younger cousin that he expected more from and not like he was talking to the Savior of the world. The outcome? He forfeited enjoying Jesus as the very Savior he preached about all those years. I did the same thing John did to the person I was serving, and I got the same kind of response... initially. But I had an advantage... I will tell you what it is at the end of this book.

Poor Stewards Are Wasters

You can spot a poor steward by the amount of waste they produce. Waste is generally all they produce. They don't see or treat people, time, resources and opportunities according to their value. They don't see, much less look for, opportunities to produce, multiply and enhance for the sake of their master or themselves. That makes it easy to waste things. If you identify as a steward and you see yourself increasingly wasting and disregarding things: time, money, etc.... and if you see yourself begin to place value and energy in things that waste time and diminish value, beware and get back on track!

One of the most important things poor stewards fail to see the value in and waste is themselves. I hate to say it, but John the Baptist demonstrates this towards the end of his life and it's a tragedy... a tragedy that worked out for me in the end, but a tragedy none the less. Look here:

> *As John's disciples were leaving, Jesus began to speak to the crowd about John: "What did you go out into the wilderness to see? A reed swayed by the wind? If not, what did you go out to see? A man dressed in fine clothes? No, those who wear fine clothes are in kings' palaces. Then what did you go out to see? A prophet? Yes, I tell you, and more than a prophet. This is the one about whom it is written: "'I will send my messenger ahead of you, who will prepare your way before you.' Truly I tell you, among those born of women there has not risen anyone greater than John the Baptist; yet whoever is least in the kingdom of heaven is greater than he. From the days of John the Baptist until now, the kingdom of heaven has been subjected to*

YWM²

> *violence, and violent people have been raiding it. For all the Prophets and the Law prophesied until John. And if you are willing to accept it, he is the Elijah who was to come. Whoever has ears, let them hear.*
>
> **Matthew 11:7-10**

Do you hear how valuable Jesus is telling everyone John is? John was a standard and a force to be reckoned with. *"There has not risen anyone greater than John the Baptist..."*

But John was a poor steward of the identity and privilege He was given through Christ Jesus. He could have demanded, by virtue of His relationship with Christ, fellowship of suffering with Christ and excellent record of stewardship to enjoy the salvation of the Lord. But instead, he sat in a prison of fear right along with his bad decision until his head was cut off.

When God told me to write about stewardship, I believed I was a the least qualified to do so. The fact that I just lost a job and a baby proved I was far from steward of the year. I told Isaiah, my husband, I quit ministry expecting him to use my announcement as an invitation to make more babies or talk about how toxic church leadership can be. Instead he said, and I quote: "How can you quit a job you didn't apply for? You were given a privilege and responsibility and you wasted it. That's stupid". Then he went back to watching his YouTube videos as he muttered, "I never heard of anything like that. Is that how anointing works? Is it everybody they gave that privilege?"

Isaiah and the Holy Spirit seemed to be working in tandem with their convicting and redirecting. *Isaiah is agreeing with the Holy Spirit. Let me not waste this experience.* And that is when it hit me. I may not have been the best steward of my clarinet, or those apartment keys, but I will steward the grace out any kingdom lesson you send my way. I am an experienced steward of God's grace and mercy.

I make a lot of big crazy mistakes. But once I learn from them, I don't waste time before I teach others, especially kids, how to make most of messy situations. I don't waste mistakes… I don't waste experiences good or bad… and I definitely don't waste grace. I'm not a waster! I'm a good steward! I can write this chapter! This must be why God keeps me in leadership everywhere I find myself. He knows it's my weakness and a place where He can show Himself strong.

In addition to ministry positions, I have resigned from a number of leadership roles. The Lord opened my eyes to this pattern I have of approaching leadership from my own strength then wondering why I'm overwhelmed and want to quit. He showed me how, in most instances I was not qualified, nor did I apply but I was consistently appointed or looked to for leadership. That's not a coincidence.

Once I received that revelation, I had to make up my mind to be a good steward of every leadership opportunity God presented me with. Doing this has proven quite profitable to me. I pray you step into such a revelation and enjoy the profitability of your stewardship in Christ in Jesus' mighty name.

The Tea: He Has a Son!

Me and John the Baptist wrote passive- aggressive messages to our leaders. Both of us had valid reasons to feel how we felt at that time. What was the difference between the outcomes of John the Baptists and my own?

I understood the value of right relationships. I repented and got back in line even when I was told by others my outcome was final and what I deserved. They were not wrong. But I went back and did everything I could to get back in place because I remembered the value of relationship. Remember when I showed you this?

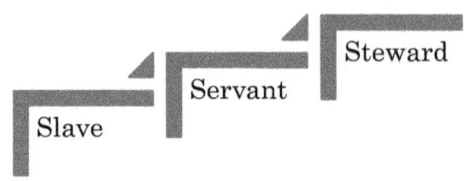

FIGURE 2: STEWARDSHIP PROGRESSION

I explained that good stewardship is our goal as Christians. But I also told you, we are worth much more. So though I made the mistake of telling my leader I had no interest in being the lead steward he'd trusted me to be, and I knew him choosing to accept my resignation was what I deserved, I decided it was wiser to remember who I was and who I was dealing with and at least make every effort to be a good steward of what was left in our relationship.

In this case, I was dealing with my spiritual father. He always told me I was a "son" in the house. If the prodigal son could make a comeback, and if my spiritual father was anything like his Father in heaven, which I knew him to be, there was always a place for restoration. So, with sonship, inheritance and honor in mind, I ignored what others said the outcome would be and stood firmly on what I knew that relationship had to offer me, one of which was redemption.

The aforementioned model of moving from slavery to stewardship will get you where you were created to be. And it is good. But thanks to Jesus, who decided we should be joint heirs, with Him, we are entitled to much more.

> [1]*Now I say, as long as the heir is a child, he does not differ at all from a slave, although he is owner of everything,* [2]*but he is under guardians and managers until the date set by the father.* [3]*So we too, when we were children, were held in bondage under the elementary principles of the world.* [4]*But when the fullness of the time came, God sent His Son, born of a woman, born under the Law,* [5]*so that He might redeem those who were under the Law, that we might receive the adoption as sons and daughters.* [6]*Because you are sons, God has sent the Spirit of His Son into our hearts, crying out, "Abba! Father!"* [7]*Therefore you are no longer a slave, but a son; and if a son, then an heir through God.*

Galatians 4:1-7

All that being said, we have a better model:

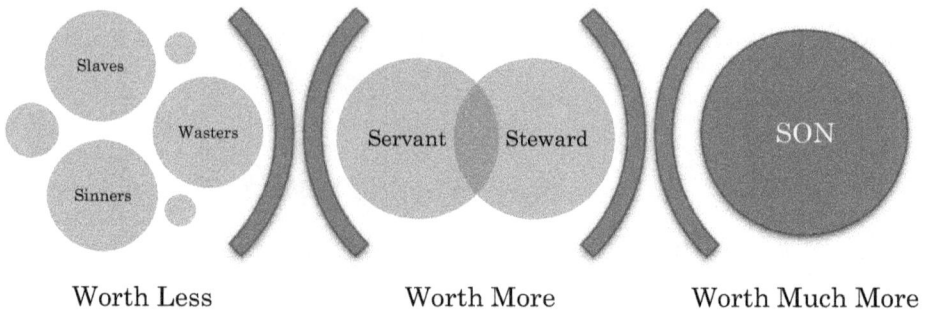

FIGURE 3: YW(M)² MODEL

Remember, I said a good steward produces and enhances things. So I did just that with the situation I found myself in. I used every spiritual resource I had not only to get it right, but to be an example for others who might let the devil tell them to quit in the place of their ministry, calling or destiny relationships.

Not only did I obtain mercy in the eyes of my leader (the Holy Spirit as well as the pastor I quit on), I also got all the blessings I could have asked for in the presence of everyone who knew how much I had messed up and was undeserving of second chances. It was very prodigal son like, only I still had my inheritance, and no pigs were ever involved.

YWM²

You Are Worth Much More

I wrote this whole book to convince you that you are valuable enough to be everything God wants you to be. I wrote it to encourage you to reproduce. But you can't be or make what you haven't become. I'm not even talking about being saved. That one is sure for you, in Jesus' name. I'm talking about being a son. I'm talking about learning how to walk around as if your Father owns the place (and He does).

Good sons are the best kinds of stewards because they take ownership of their Father's affairs. Sons take correction without offense knowing the Father has their best interest at heart. Should a son stray away, there will always be a rejoicing upon his return. A steward can stray and come back too, but there will always be a question mark where he is concerned. If a steward does well, he will surely gain a reward. But a son's reward is an inheritance, that is everything the Father has. I think that's worth more and it's what God wants for you. Once you have enjoyed being the son of a good, good Father, no one will need to coerce you to keep the legacy going.

I have shared over 150 pages of my personal business and other stories with you because you are worth it. In fact, you are worth much more. I can't put in words how good it feels to be loved by God as if you were His only begotten Son. This is what He desires for you.

Princess Sheri

I used to teach Rhema School in a Redeemed Christian Churches of God parish. My Head of Department, Dcn. Smatt, used to call me "Princess". He always greeted and counseled me as such. I thought it was just because I was the only one among us in her twenties teaching Sunday School to grown men and women until one day, we were having a serious conversation about a major decision I was thinking of making and He still called me Princess, but the tone hit me a bit differently. *This man really thinks I'm a princess,* I remember thinking.

There was something about the way He said it that I suddenly believed it. Maybe it was the content of the conversation. Actually, I know what it was. He called it out as if it were my title. He triggered me into respecting myself as royalty, and not like I was still a newborn in Christ just trying to get it right. He spoke to me as someone who had an inheritance coming soon… someone with a reputation to think about.

As he counseled me on my decision- he did not tell me what to do or judge, no. He just made sure I had all the information I needed as someone who was responsible for the affairs of her Father's kingdom. That was a game changer for me. I learned I was both fragile and powerful. I was so valuable; I was in need of protection and wise counsel. I was so powerful, my decisions impacted both earthly and divine realms. Everything I was and did mattered. They always had.

In Conclusion

Never give up on yourself because it's not about you. You were created as a very tiny piece of a greater master plan. But you are a piece that the plans of God cannot do without because of what you can produce.

Like I said in the beginning, you are the Riches and Glory of God. This book is over, but I pray this is just the beginning for you.

Honors

The next semi-chapter is a hybrid of the "Afterword" and "Acknowledgement" sections of this book. It's designed to give you a final word- mostly in the form of stories, of course. I also wrote it to show the world exactly how I went from believing I was unlovable to knowing I am loved in such an abundance; the pages of this book could never contain the names of everyone God used to bring me into the "Much More" side of my life here on earth.

You're Blessed, forever.

Aftermath.

Simon, Simon, Satan has asked to sift all of you as wheat. ³² But I have prayed for you, Simon, that your faith may not fail. And when you have turned back, strengthen your brothers.
Luke 22:31-32

I didn't think so at first, but me and Peter had much in common. Do you know what *sift* means? Google the definition. He didn't just want to kill us. He wanted to shred us to pieces so we lose sight and access to the best parts of ourselves. Then kill us. I used to think every spiritual attack I encountered was indicative of the fact that I was not strong enough or worthy enough to carry out life on this side of eternity.

Now I know that I am so valuable, not an ounce of my past, pain or even mistakes can be wasted. But I didn't figure all this out on my own. This chapter is dedicated to honor a few of the people who are part of my equation.

Bread + Bed Breakers

Isaiah Asuoha is the first person on earth I never hid from. He met me at the lowest, most erratic time of my life and pursued me anyway. He pursued even after I denied him three times, like Peter did Jesus, not realizing he was part of my salvation plan until it was almost too late. Isaiah has sacrificed many things for the sake of my comfort, healing and destiny. He taught me things I didn't know I needed to know, helping me change negative habits and behaviors I thought I was bound to forever. We break bread and beds (inside joke) together regularly. I am so grateful for you and what we've produced.

They Say I Look Like My Mother

My mother was the first person to recognize the grace on my life. I think she tried to preserve it by sending me to stay with my uncle and grandparents where I would learn and gain everything I couldn't with her.

My mother is a 4"8 army veteran with trauma she seldom discusses if ever. She trained us like soldiers. There are times she might feel guilty about her role in some of my childhood trauma, but she taught me *there is therefore no condemnation for those who are in Christ Jesus* (Romans 8:1). She repented and moved on.

YWM²

She was walking down the street one day (during my Keisha years), and someone thought she was me. I don't know what exactly they said to her, but it was enough to let her know that the years she spent waking us up for church ...taking us to all the vacation Bible schools... the prayer meetings, didn't seem to be paying off. Maybe she felt like all the negative things in her life that she tried to protect us from were overriding everything she tried to fix.

We always think we can fix and heal and do things on our own. She was partly right if she felt working all the over- time to give us a better life and not sleeping for days so we wouldn't miss church was a waste of her time. But I think at some point she realized the magnitude of the spiritual strongholds and generational curses we were up against, and she made us memorize scripture upon scripture and gave me access to her library.

So while I did take wrong turns in life, I was protected and preserved by God's word that I hid in my heart and learned the power of writing while reading all her Christian books.

Thank you, Mom, for your labor of love and for making me memorize Psalm 24, Psalm 100, Psalm 23,

Ephesians 6 (I used this one as a frame of reference every time you brought out the extension cord, Mr. Spoon, or whatever inanimate object you were going to use to subdue my flesh. Once it finally worked, I learned to use it in every hostile situation I found myself in) and most importantly, Romans 8:28-39.

King's Kid

I don't know how she learned legacy. Her childhood was also quite brutal, and she was not as exposed to the Word of God as a child the way she made sure we were. She taught me the books of the Bible. She taught me how to serve and sow. She taught me how to enjoy the fat of the land. Most importantly she taught me what faith is. She is the one who first exposed me to the power of covenant. My Grandfather introduced me to calling, purpose and the ministry of teaching and raising leaders and world changers.

I am grateful beyond words for my grandparents, Dr. Willie and Sherion Weston, for demonstrating unconditional love and patience, exposing me to calling and keeping me safe. Grandmother and Grandfather, thank you for telling me stories, showing me how to have fun and enjoy life and most importantly for loving me unconditionally and letting me know I was a King's Kid.

Sisters! And Brother!

I cried for two years over the two brothers I lost, Wayne Jones and Samuel Feliciano. I thank God for their impact on my life and for helping me value my siblings who are still alive. William Chris, Adrianna Sophia and Carmina Cherie, thank you all for giving me my first opportunity to be a good steward. I probably could have done a much better job...but considering the circumstances... thank you for unconditional love and trust in me as your big sister.

My brother, Chris inspired me to get my degree in clinical counseling. I remember being so young and hearing they wanted to put him on medication for hyperactivity. I wanted to understand why, and this pushed me to go to college becoming the first in my family to earn a degree from a university. I also remember thinking I was the family genius until I found out how high his IQ was. Everything about my brother is off the charts. Chris, I think the most important thing you did was help me see that there was a world bigger than me and my perceived problems. Thank you. I pray you become and receive everything God has for you. You are more than worth it.

My younger sister, the Dreamer, was born with a very smart mouth. But unlike most, she has the brains and voice to back it up. She became the lead singer of our band, The Peculiar People, at the age of five. She was the only one of us who skipped a grade and didn't get sent back to their original grade after just one week like her older sister, Muffin did in first grade. Without knowing it, she inspired me to stay in school and become the best I could be educationally for the sake of helping people heal. She is the best nurse I know. Sister, walk in the fullness of your worth and the anointing. I swear you have the anointing for healing. You were the first partaker of what it could look like given the miracles of life you have experienced and your testimonies. Carmina Cherie, thank you for spoiling your nieces, proofreading and all that you do.

I told you all earlier about my "cry" baby sister, Adrianna. Thank you for crying out and keeping us all connected. As long as you keep stewarding relationships the way you do, you will never run out of business ideas, and you will always have more than enough. I have seen you wear many hats, but you and I know you have more hats to wear. I can't wait! Thank you for all you do and are!

Help and Assistance

One day, my stepfather took me on a car ride after I did or said something stupid during my "Keisha" days. He is known for long lectures. But there are two that meant a lot. One of those times was this time in his car, "You know that I love you, right?" It was one of the most awkward moments of my life, right up there with the time he said I should call him "Dad". I don't recall how I responded. I had never heard those words from anyone but my grandmother as far as I could remember. The other lecture I'll always remember is when he wanted me to clean the kitchen to his standard. He gave me an analogy of how cleaning the kitchen should be like writing a sentence. Sweeping was the period. Guillermo Feliciano, aka Felice, knowing you knew what was important to me and for me mattered and supersedes the awkward. Thank you for all you do.

I was at me church and came across a bunch of books called *Forgiving Forward*. It was a good read and I wished I had a part in the editing process. The author of the book came to minister at my church one day boldly declaring that if we didn't want to, we didn't need to wear glasses because healing was there for us. I tried it, but I looked strange without my glasses... or so I assumed... I don't know. I couldn't see very well. A few weeks later, my fellow deaconess and prescription glasses-wearer came to church, no contacts and no glasses! She gave the testimony of how the man of God's message impacted her.

Every time Pst. Felix Bamirin came to minister at our church after that, I made sure I got my testimony. Pastor Coach, I am glad we have the opportunity to cross paths. Thank you for always attending to me with all you have going. Thanks for trusting me and 7th Seal with your publications. Thanks for pioneering Light + Life Coaching, it's been a blessing for me. Your family and church family are blessed.

Cherie Animashaun, it's a privilege to know you and work with you. I could not have selected a better right hand in this editing business of ours. I don't think I need to tell you how much of an advantage you are. You are blessed and so is everything that has to do with you, forever.

YWM²

Family

I am grateful for my family, the Weston's, my aunts, uncle, cousins and in-laws. My uncle, my mother's brother and the one she sent me to stay with one summer, made being a writer, director and overall creative accessible to me. Thank you, Pastor W.L. Weston.

I am grateful for the Asuoha's who welcomed a foreigner into their family. If they judged me, I don't know because I have felt nothing but love and acceptance from their side. My mother- in- law was named well. Her worth is more than rubies. If Proverbs 31 was a person, its Eunice Asuoha. She has favor everywhere she goes for a reason. Thank you, Mama, for trusting me with your son. Thank you for raising my children to my standard and better while I "work and type all day" as you say. Thank you for every day you stand at the stove ensuring everyone is fed. Thank you for loving me and not making me feel bad because I can't make eba. I do not deserve you, but I am only able to move forward in destiny because God knew I needed you. Imela, O.

Mama

So it shall be, while My glory passes by, that I will put you in the cleft of the rock and will cover you with My hand while I pass by.

Sheri Asuoha

Exodus 33:22

When my biological mother was trying to get me to walk in the anointing that she felt she saw upon my life, I was comfortably bound by trauma. More than once, she tried to make me sing a song in front of the whole church. It was a song about Moses being told by God to go to Egypt and let His people go. I wouldn't sing that song or any song. I stood in front of those church people like a statue. She brought me the Prince of Egypt soundtrack years later and would remind me of how I refused to obey the instruction she gave me to sing the song of Moses, an instruction she believed was in line with my destiny. *Why the heck would I want to be like Moses?* I thought to myself.

Years later, I met Rev. Dr. Adesola Babalola. Anyone who has ever listened to her pray must know Exodus 33:22. In this scripture, God gives Moses what he asked for while keeping him safe. He gives Moses a privilege he hasn't dished out since Adam messed up. The same Moses who was fearful, violent and tongue-tied was the leader God desired to lead his people and speak to face to face.

YWM²

Rev. Dr. Adesola Babalola became my spiritual mother. Before she became my pastor, she met me having marital problems. My husband was wearing me out! Every other woman of God- I'm talking Nigerian women- pastors- said I should be careful of Isaiah or drop him as soon as I could. He was going to use me for papers and leave me and so on. Not Rev. Dr. Adesola Babalola. She told me to cook him a meal and kneel before him so he could bless me. *Now I just told her he cursed me out. She knows I can't cook. But she wants me to make him a meal and believes he will bless me? This lady is way too culture-bound to understand how impractical these instructions she gave me really are*, I thought… but only for about ten minutes. Then, unlike I did when my mother instructed me to sing the prophetic Moses song, I obeyed.

Since the day I followed her impractical advise, Isaiah has not stopped blessing me. We just made 12 years of marriage. Mama, I was right about you being culture-bound, but wrong about the culture in question. Thank you for being of the kingdom. Thanks for sharing your grace with me. Thank you for teaching us the power of purity and humility and that God's grace really is sufficient for us.

Sheri Asuoha

My Beloved

When I was pregnant with Eden, I walked across the stage, belly out, to become the first person in my family to obtain a Masters' Degree or any degree for that matter.

When I was pregnant with Trinity, I reached a peak in my career and was so closed to obtaining my doctorate before I eventually gave up. My mother in the Lord and I were discussing something one day after that.

"Oh," she said as if we were not just talking about something else, "I know why you should not quit your doctoral program," I did not have the heart to tell her I was already dismissed and had no motivation to contest the decision.

"Why is that? I don't need the prestige and you don't really need a doctorate to be a therapist."

"Think about Eden. Think of Trinity and your children to come. You don't know what they will be in life. For the sake of their destiny you need to finish what you start. Maybe they will need to be doctors. At least if they see you with your doctorate, they will have someone to look up to and that will make it easier for them. If you go as far as you can go, then they can go much further." *Now you tell me,* I thought to myself.

After I had AnaiahMishael, I tried a few times to get into a doctoral program while balancing life and finances. I finally got into the right program. God opened doors for acceptance, financial resources, grace and more making it impossible for me to ever quit again. I have spent much of Anaiah's life on earth rounding up my doctoral program.

Thank you, girls, for being part of my process. Thank you for your patience. Thank you for every time you run to meet me at the door when I finally come home. Thank you for starting ETA services to bring me snacks while I was working, reading and writing. Thanks for being my biggest cheerleaders and helpers. Thank you for letting me and Daddy push you to be your best. Thanks for making it easy for us to become our best while you rather us spend time playing family games with you, that you may have access to everything God desires for you under the sun. Please remember that all we do, we do with your destinies in mind. You're worth far more than I can ever give you, that's why we commend you to God. I decree and declare you will remain ever in His presence until He returns. Each of you will become everything He planned for you under the sun, in Jesus' name.

Papa

When God does His things, He does them exceedingly in abundance. I remember the day that I told God I was ready to go all the way. I was in my living room. Isaiah was at work. Eden was in our bedroom with her purple pacifier. I was sitting on my couch, on Facebook and I stood up suddenly and shouted, "God, I'm ready to give you everything!! My time… even what I value the most!" What did I value most back then, you ask? Eden, my precious firstborn? Close, but no. My marriage? No. I was referring to my social media platforms.

I had gathered quite the following on Facebook posting pictures of my wild, drunken adventures. I always had a cup in my hand. Many people loved the deep and funny things I posted. They enjoyed my erotic, rated-X poems. Yes. I was ready to give all that up to post scriptures and stuff about Jesus like the old people on Facebook. I no longer cared how lame and offensive my friends and followers found it. I then prayed, not out loud, *Lord it would be nice if I had someone I could follow or who could mentor me to do what I think You want me to do.* Lots of people in the Bible had someone like that to help them on their journey.

God reminded me that the reason I made the decision to surrender all was because of a post I saw on Facebook by a man I did not know. I knew he went to my church. That's all. Days later, I made the announcement on Facebook that there would be a change in my content. Only one person responded. The guy I did not know. It turns out he wrote lots of things about Jesus. I thought I should encourage him so he wouldn't stop writing… and so he can like the next Christian post I made. I liked a few of his blogs. Occasionally, I had comments and questions and he always responded.

It's been 12 years since then and he never stopped responding. He has taken his time to read countless drafts of books I never finished. He has trusted me to edit and write for him for over a decade now. He provoked the start of my editing company. Then he provoked me to take it seriously. He would say, "You're not a novice anymore. You don't do things for free. Let people see clearly the value of what you are doing for them. You are not just correcting grammar. You are giving them much more. So charge much more." If you are a beloved 7th Seal client, and you see my rates rise, he is the reason why (smiles).

I quit on him several times, but he never gave up on me. In fact, he poured the oil on my head and transferred every grace he ever received from God into my life, provoking my calling that has led to children and adults throughout Illinois and all over the internet receiving healing, being delivered from dangerous habits, being connected to their calling, being delivered from situations of trafficking and more. I have designed and commissioned life changing programs and initiatives because he decided not to give up on me.

Besides all the spiritual gifts he's given me, every now again, if he travels, as apostles do, he will always bring me something back (my mother taught me that was the sign of a good father). Also, there were times he learned I needed gas money and was ashamed to ask or he just decided to bless me for working on his books or whatever. I would always say, "Aww! Thank you, Sir, but you didn't have to do that," to which he would look me in the eye and reply, "Please. You are worth much more,". Hence the name of this book.

All that said: To my pastor and father in destiny, thank you. It is a privilege to drink from your cistern, Sir.

Kingdom Kids, Kingdom Future and their Teachers

Every kingdom kid and teacher inspires me regularly. My biological children and the next generation are safe because you exist. Kingdom Future, you make God smile. He knows the world is better because He has you are here.

Elohim

Holy are you Lord. There is no one like you. Holy are you Lord...

You have kept me all this while.

You have kept me all this while.

You have shown me Your love

My world can't deny

Your tender mercies, I enjoy every day.

There is no one like you...

I did not write that song, my Papa did. But I am sure it was my heart's cry that he heard before he knew he had to write it. That song is the story of my life and the summary of every book I'll ever write. To my Father, the Most High, Your love for me remains forever unmatched. You're my value and advantage. I can't do or be without You. Thank you, Daddy.

{Afterword}

I have been a part of Sheri's journey as her pastor and father in Christ for close to twelve years. I had the privilege of reading *YWM²* as it was being written. Knowing what I knew about her journey thus far, it gladdened my heart to watch prophecy unfold as this book came to completion.

I met Sheri shortly after I transitioned to the U.S in 2009. I knew writing was a major part of her assignment on the earth but getting the exact thing to write about took her years to figure out. I remember so many times she would share her desire to write her own book as she was helping so many others write and publish theirs. I would tell her just keep walking in the anointing and calling she carried because her time would surely come, and she would know exactly what to write.

If it takes you years to understand what God requires of you, do not relent. Find out what God has placed you on earth to do. Train, pass every test and do it well. I am so glad, Sheri got it right.

Sheri Asuoha

In *YWM²*, Sheri places her testimonies in story form as a destiny resource for you and anyone who reads this book. They are testimonies of overcoming and proof that, indeed, "...all things work together for the good of those who love Jesus" (Romans 8:28). Part of the "all things" that must work together for you includes your past. The great thing about this book is that it helps one to make sense of every life experience. No matter how seemingly bad or irrelevant the devil makes some parts of your life seem, when you are clear about your value, you understand that nothing about your life can be wasted, not even your past.

Sheri has placed close to ten years of Christian book editing into skillfully writing this book in a manner that lets it reach everyone, especially young minds who may just be starting out on their journey.

Maybe your journey has started out strangely. Trust you are destined for glory. Please, after you have been blessed, take the time to reproduce your experience in somebody else. Let people know that no matter the cost, they must learn they are of eternal value and begin to live accordingly.

- Rev. 'Sola Babalola

{About The Author}

Sherilynn "Sheri" Asuoha is a Christian. She lives out her faith with her husband, Isaiah and their three daughters, EdenSophia, TrinityElise, & AnaiahMishael. A Christian and writer since childhood, Sheri is Founder and Chief Editor at 7th Seal Advantage, LLC, a Christian editing and publishing service established in 2012. She serves as a Managing Director at Emmaus, a nonprofit shedding light and solutions to the problem of commercial sexual exploitation and human trafficking.

Sheri double majored in psychology and social work at Lewis University and holds a Master's in Clinical Counseling from the Chicago School of Professional Psychology. She hopes to complete her Doctorate in Education at Bradley University in December 2021. Sheri is a Licensed Clinical Professional Counselor in the State of Illinois. She is an ordained minister at Kingdom Pathway Church, where something happens that doesn't happen anywhere else. She is also the author of *Faith Classic*, co-written with Pastor Dele Osunmakinde.

www.ingramcontent.com/pod-product-compliance
Lightning Source LLC
Chambersburg PA
CBHW022104090426
42743CB00008B/715